Thomas Finlayson Henderson

The Casket Letters and Mary Queen of Scots

With appendices

Thomas Finlayson Henderson

The Casket Letters and Mary Queen of Scots
With appendices

ISBN/EAN: 9783337323684

Printed in Europe, USA, Canada, Australia, Japan

Cover: Foto ©ninafisch / pixelio.de

More available books at **www.hansebooks.com**

THE CASKET LETTERS

AND

MARY QUEEN OF SCOTS

WITH APPENDICES

BY

T. F. HENDERSON

EDINBURGH
ADAM AND CHARLES BLACK
1889

PREFACE.

The 'Casket Letters' controversy—important though the issues involved in it may be—has latterly been regarded by many as practically futile, the supposition being that no evidence is now obtainable adequate to justify a very definite conclusion on one side or the other. The character latterly assumed by the controversy in this country has afforded some ground for this prevailing opinion. It is only on the Continent—and especially in Germany—that the importance and significance of the discoveries of original versions of the letters have been recognised. In the present volume an endeavour is made to show that within recent years substantial progress has been made towards a definite conclusion; but the chief reason for its publication is the discovery of the vital evidence contained in Morton's Declaration.

CONTENTS.

CHAPTER I.
INTRODUCTORY.

	PAGE
Historical Interest of the Casket Problem,	1
Mary's Prominent Place in Scottish History,	3
The Regent Moray, Cecil, and Elizabeth,	3
Mr. Skelton's Middle Position as to Mary's Guilt,	4
Mary's Attitude towards Bothwell,	6
Mr. Swinburne's Alternative,	8
Bearing of the Casket Evidence,	9
The Regent Moray's Position,	10

CHAPTER II.
PRODUCTION OF THE LETTERS IN SCOTLAND.

Bothwell and Mary after "Kirk-o'-Field,"	12
Discovery of the Casket—Morton's Declaration,	13
The Privy Council Reference,	13
Throckmorton's Statement,	14
Were the Letters produced at Lochleven?	15
De Silva and the Regent Moray,	16
Drury's Statement,	17
Were the Letters produced on 4th December?	19
Professor Schiern's Ingenious Theory,	20
Hosack's supposed Discovery,	21
Were the Letters produced in the Scottish Parliament?	24

CHAPTER III.

THE PRODUCTION OF THE LETTERS IN ENGLAND.

	PAGE
Mary's Flight to England,	27
Negotiations of the Regent Moray,	27
Commission at York,	28
Character and Powers of the Commission,	29
The Letters shown privately,	30
Was the French Version produced at York?	31
The Westminster Conference,	32
Declaration of the Scottish Commissioners,	34
Examination of the Letters,	35
Criticism of Hosack adopted by Professor Schiern and Mr. Skelton,	36
The Charge of Carelessness—the Persons at Fault,	38
The Two Minutes,	39
Tendency of the Weight of Evidence,	40
Return of the Scottish Commissioners with the Casket,	40

CHAPTER IV.

THE PUBLICATION OF THE LETTERS.

Disappearance of the Letters,	42
By whom were they destroyed?	43
By Mary's Accusers?	45
By the Marian Party?	46
By James VI.?	46
Buchanan's *Detection*,	47
Mr. Skelton on Cecil and Buchanan,	48
Was there a "Transparent Mystification"?	49
Cecil's "Obscure Activity,"	50

CONTENTS. ix

CHAPTER V.

THE CONTROVERSY.

	PAGE
Goodall's Demonstration,	51
Hosack's Modification of Goodall's Theory,	53
Mr. Skelton's Exposition of the Theory,	53
Hosack's Discoveries,	54
Compromising Expressions in Letter 4,	55
Did Darnley know French?	56
Belief of Lennox in the "Handwrite,"	58
Could the Letters not have been sent to Bothwell?	59
Hazardous Character of Hosack's Theory,	60
Letter 2 and Crawford's Declaration,	61
Baron de Lettenhove's Discovery at Hatfield,	62
Dr. Bresslau's Criticism of the Letters,	63
Mr. Skelton's Latest Opinions,	63
Mr. Skelton and Markham Thorpe,	64
Professor Mandell Creighton's Views,	65
The Editors of the Hatfield Calendar,	65
Demolition of the Modified Goodall Theory,	66
Mr. Skelton and Recent Continental Writers,	67
Recent German Theories,	67
The supposed "Manipulations,"	68
Dr. Bresslau's Conclusions,	69
How far these Conclusions are warranted,	70

CHAPTER VI.

LETTER 2.

Peculiar Structure of the Letter,	72
An "Unaccountable Intimation,"	73
Mr. Froude's Estimate,	73
Mr. Skelton's Opinion,	73

CONTENTS.

	PAGE
Hosack's Criticism,	74
The "Coarseness of Tone,"	75
Minute References in the Letter,	76
Was it originally written in French?	77
Examples of the Influence of a French Original,	77
The Letter and Crawford's Declaration,	82
Was there "Collusion"?	83
Was the Letter partly forged from Crawford's Statements?	85
Could the Letter have been written from Glasgow?	86
In what Sense the Evidence is Negative,	89

CHAPTER VII.
MORTON'S DECLARATION.

Discovery of the Declaration,	90
Its Exhaustive Statements,	90
The "Sichting" of the Documents,	91
The Witnesses to the "Sichting,"	92
The Catholic Nobles,	93
Testimony of Atholl,	94
Testimony of Lord Home,	94
Testimony of other Nobles,	94
What the Testimony proves,	95
The "most Notable Witness,"	95
Maitland of Lethington and Queen Mary,	96
Morton and Maitland,	96
Maitland's Silence,	97
Was Maitland the Forger?	98
Mr. Skelton's Past and Present Views,	99
Mr. Skelton on Morton,	99
Mr. Skelton's Vindication of Maitland,	100
Maitland and Darnley—the "Verdict of not proven,"	101
Mr. Skelton's Dilemma,	102
Morton's Declaration and Moray's Receipt,	103
Conditions essential to the Forgery Theory,	104

CHAPTER VIII.

CONCLUSION.

	PAGE
Mary's Denial,	105
Mary's Silence,	106
Attitude of France and Spain,	107
The Catholics and the Murder of Darnley,	108
The Protestant Nobles of Scotland and the Murder,	108
The only Excuse for their Conduct,	109
The Regent Moray and his Sister,	109
Elizabeth's Treatment of Mary,	109

APPENDICES.

APPENDIX A.

Morton's Declaration,	113

APPENDIX B.

Lord Home's Deposition,	117
Deposition of William Kirkaldy of Grange,	119

APPENDIX C.

CASKET DOCUMENTS.

MARRIAGE CONTRACTS.

The First Contract,	121
The Second Contract,	122

THE CASKET LETTERS.

LETTER I.

Scots and English Translations,	124
Latin and French Translations,	125

LETTER II.

	PAGE
Scots and English Translations,	127
Latin and French Translations,	141

LETTER III.

Original French Version and Scots Translation,	156

LETTER IV.

Original French Version, and French and Latin Translations,	159
Scots and English Translations,	163

LETTER V.

Original French Version, and French and Scots Translations,	165

LETTER VI.

Original French Version, and French Translation,	167
Scots and English Translations,	169

LETTER VII.

Scots and French Translations,	171

LETTER VIII.

Scots and French Translations,	172

LETTER IX.

"French Sonnets,"	173

APPENDIX D.

I. Act of Secret Council,	177
II. Act of Parliament anent the Retention of our Souverane Motheris Person,	182
III. Journal of the Proceedings of the Lords of the Privy Council of England, 14th day of December 1568,	186
IV. Journal of the Proceedings of the Lords of the Privy Council of England, 15th day of December 1568,	189

THE CASKET LETTERS AND MARY QUEEN OF SCOTS.

CHAPTER I.

INTRODUCTORY.

As a strictly literary problem, the question of the authenticity of the Casket Letters, attributed to Mary Queen of Scots, can scarcely claim to rank on an equality with that of the authorship of the Letters of Junius. On the other hand, it greatly exceeds it in importance as a historical problem. The historical issues involved in the authorship that may be assigned to the Letters of Junius are of comparatively minor moment, but in the case of the Casket Letters they are the main matter. The Iron Mask problem, like that of the Casket Letters, is essentially a historical problem; but nevertheless the historical issues involved in it are not the main, or, necessarily, an important matter. Both these problems are flavoured by a strong human interest, but the one interest differs widely in character from the other. Both imply historical research, but they have scarcely one other historical characteristic in common. The Iron Mask problem is the more awesome and mysterious, and affords much wider scope for ingenious theory and learned historical plodding, but this is mainly because the character of the solution is by the conditions of the problem a matter of extremely wide uncertainty. From the nature of the case, it is impossible to predict what exact amount of historical importance may attach to the solution of the problem, although that importance is not likely, on any supposition, to be exceptional. The interest of the problem is thus only in an indirect sense historical. Apart from the curiosity awakened regarding the individuality of one whose identity was concealed with such persistent and careful precaution, the problem is almost as purely speculative and intellectual as a problem in chess or mathematics. The man in the Iron Mask is supposed to have been a political prisoner of high and probably royal rank, but the fascination of the problem is due chiefly to the fact that his personality is unknown. In the case of the Casket Letters, the uncertainty of the solution is limited by the fact that only one of two conclusions is possible. The range of inquiry is very definite and distinct, and the question is merely one of forgery. The forgery, if it was a forgery, is perhaps worthy to be regarded as the most daring, ingenious, complicated, and skilfully performed forgery on record; but, apart from this, the Casket Letters question has a special and indubitable pre-eminence over other forgery questions, from the important historical issues involved in its solution. The historical interest is here the predominant one. So far as it relates to Mary Queen of Scots, the solution of the problem may afford some special information regarding the character and conduct of a very remarkable and striking personality—one whose romantic and chequered career and pitiable fate have a peculiar fascination for the mere student of human nature as distinguished from the student of history; but it can never be forgotten that Mary was one of the most prominent political figures of her time. She lived during the crisis of a great religious and political conflict; she represented the forlorn hope of the old Catholic faith in Scotland; she was the occasion of a prolonged and bitter civil war. The passions aroused by the conflict are not even yet altogether spent and dead; the echoes of the old sectarian watchwords are still heard; the partisanship which caused such deeds of cruelty and crime three centuries ago is even now more than a memory or a tradition. Moreover, in the solution of the problem, the characters of other persons are involved besides Mary; and, in fact, it will be seen in the sequel that the question concerns still more directly and vitally the character and conduct of her political opponents, including both the Regent Moray and his supporters, and Queen Elizabeth and her advisers.

To establish the genuineness of the Casket Letters is necessarily to establish that Mary was a co-conspirator with Bothwell in the murder of her husband; for, notwithstanding the attempted apology of Bishop Leslie, based on the fact that the murder is not there referred to in so many words, the expressions in the letters are not consistent with an innocent purpose, or with the theory that she brought Darnley to Edinburgh in order to facilitate the obtaining of a divorce. Apart even from other corroborative evidence, the evidence of the letters, if their genuineness be admitted, is sufficient to establish her guilt. Inasmuch, however, as her entire innocence is not consistent with other evidence, it can scarcely be affirmed that the problem of the genuineness of the letters has an absolutely vital bearing on the character of Mary. Mr. Skelton, who does not admit the genuineness of the letters, and who may be reckoned one of the most distinguished and ingenious defenders of Mary in this country, has taken no pains to conceal his contempt for what he terms the "theory of the ecclesiastics"—that Mary, during the whole progress of the plot against Darnley's life, was "innocent as a child, immaculate as a saint." He is unable to adopt a more friendly attitude towards her than that of an apologizer, and is compelled to attempt the assumption of a middle position—that she was neither wholly innocent nor wholly guilty;

that, ignorant of the details and method of the plot, she only vaguely guessed that it was in progress, and failed merely in firmly and promptly forbidding its execution. But in a case of murder a middle position—a position of even partial indifference—is, except in very peculiar circumstances, well-nigh impossible; in the case of a wife's attitude to the murder of her husband, the limit of impossibility is still more nearly approached; but when the wife possesses such exceptional courage, fertility of resource, and strength of will as were possessed by Mary, the impossibility may be regarded as absolute. Besides, as a matter of fact, Mary was not indifferent in the matter. She had long regarded her husband's conduct with antipathy and indignation; she did not conceal her eager desire to be delivered from the yoke of marriage to him; and she had abundant reasons, many of which were justifiable, for this desire. By admitting that Mary was not wholly ignorant of the plot, Mr. Skelton inevitably exposes himself to the following dilemma. If, on the one hand, it be said that Mary and Darnley had become fully reconciled at Glasgow: that his illness and contrition had aroused her pity and awakened old and slumbering feelings of affection, and that she brought him with her to Edinburgh in order that for the future they might live together as husband and wife; then, knowing that his life was in peril, she would have taken prompt measures to avert the danger, and would not, above all, have permitted the free access to his lodgings of such a "glorious, rash, and hazardous" personage as she knew Bothwell from old experience to be. If, on the other hand, she was not sincerely reconciled to her husband when she tended him with such watchful care, both during the journey from Glasgow and at Kirk-o'-Field, she could have had no other reason for bringing him to Kirk-o'-Field, except to aid the designs of the conspirators. Her attitude towards the chief conspirator was not of a merely passive kind. It was not only that she made no effort to discover the murderer, but she used every safe effort to prevent his detection and condemnation. In her letters to the Archbishop of Glasgow she endeavoured to represent the plot as one directed rather against her own life than that of her husband. Moreover, the final conclusion of the matter was, that she married the murderer. She knew sufficiently well that the almost universal opinion of the people pointed to Bothwell as the main conspirator, and yet from the first her attitude to him remained, to say the least, as friendly as before; he did not become in any degree a less favoured companion, nor did his influence in her counsels suffer any diminution. Her best friends, when they mentioned to her with hesitation the rumours that she intended to marry Bothwell, warned her against taking such a fatal step, but her only answer was that matters were not yet "that far agaitwait."[1] The excuses

---

[1] Sir James Melville's *Memoirs*, p. 177.

that have been made on the score of broken or uncertain health can scarcely be regarded seriously, for Mary, notwithstanding a very dangerous illness in October, had made her journey to Glasgow in midwinter, and also remained late at a ball on the very eve of the murder. If she was engaged in such a conspiracy, no doubt anxiety, and perhaps remorse, might affect to some extent her health and spirits. That spells of perhaps somewhat artificial gaiety should be succeeded by fits of depression, or even of hysterics, was at least as consistent with guilt as with innocence. There is no evidence of anything approaching mental prostration, and no symptom that her presence of mind had deserted her. Severe mental conflict there probably was, and, it may be, some halting between two opinions, but all through the crisis her mental faculties were alert and keen. Her letters addressed to the Archbishop of Glasgow, and to Lennox, are all remarkable specimens of feminine tact, and their skilful fencing is wholly directed towards one purpose—that of parrying awkward suggestions as to the means which should be employed to avenge the murder. The question as to whether Mary was really in love with Bothwell is a comparatively minor one, for she could scarcely have been blind to the main motive which actuated Bothwell in carrying out the plot. Undoubtedly the evidence — apart even from the Casket Letters — favours the supposition that she was in love with him, rather than the supposition that she married him unwillingly. At any rate, he claimed his reward, and she granted him the reward he claimed. The fatal weakness, indeed, of all such arguments as are used to establish either Mary's absolute or partial innocence of the murder is, that they do not harmonize with the leading traits of her disposition. She was possessed of altogether exceptional decision and force of will; she was remarkably wary and acute; and she was a match for almost any of her contemporaries in the art of diplomacy. She was not one to be concussed into a course of action to which she had any strong aversion, and in all matters vitally affecting herself was in the habit of using her own independent judgment. Her conduct during the three months succeeding the murder can, however, only be regarded as consistent with her innocence, on the supposition, to use the cogent words of Mr. Swinburne, that "this conduct was a tissue of such dastardly imbecility, such heartless irresolution, and such brainless inconsistency, as for ever to dispose of her time-honoured claim to the credit of intelligence and courage."

The bearing of the evidence of the Casket Letters on the guilt of Mary is thus in a sense, and as matters have turned out, subordinate. Up to the present time her guilt has been more manifest than the genuineness of the letters. The principal historians—Hume, Robertson, Malcolm Laing, Mignet, Hill Burton, Froude—who before the publication of

Hosack's volume in 1869 supported the theory of her guilt, accepted the letters as genuine, but in this they were to some extent influenced by the supposed strength of the other evidence for her guilt. Since the publication of Hosack's volume, some who have no doubt of her guilt either reject the evidence of the letters or regard it with strong suspicion. For those who assert her innocence—and they are by no means few in number—the question of the genuineness of the letters is, however, of course vital; and any new evidence bearing on this point is necessarily regarded by them with anxiety. To those who accept the other evidence as conclusive, the question of the genuineness of the letters can be regarded with comparative unconcern; but in view of the large number who do not share their opinions, the additional corroboration of their conclusions, afforded by the letters, is not to be despised. They, if genuine, also supply important information regarding the motives which actuated Mary in consenting to the murder, and vividly exhibit the varying and tumultuous emotions by which she was agitated during the progress of the conspiracy. On the other hand, to prove that they are entire and complete forgeries does not tend inherently to weaken the other evidence against her. If insufficient without being supplemented by the letters, then to prove the forgery would only remove corroborative support; and if sufficient without support, the evidence would remain sufficient if the support were withdrawn. It is, moreover, a peculiarity of the case, that adequate motives exist for the forgery even on the supposition that Mary was guilty. When the Casket Documents were produced, the evidence for her guilt was certainly not so legally sufficient and undeniable as it is now. Time has fully disclosed much that was then only suspected or only partially visible. Supposing, also, that the evidence available to the Regent Moray had been sufficient, without the corroboration of the Casket Letters, to secure the conviction of a lesser personage than a sovereign; or even sufficient in the eyes of the majority of the Scottish nation to justify the condemnation of their queen, it might not have been sufficient to silence the scruples or remonstrances of Elizabeth. In any case, it was chiefly circumstantial evidence. Several of the nobles who supported Moray, if not Moray himself, were supposed to have been more or less directly involved in the murder; or to have given it, by the passive attitude they had adopted, their "manifest consent." Had the circumstantial evidence been narrowly examined, awkward secrets might have been brought to light. The direct palpable evidence of the letters would render the examination of this evidence unnecessary. Thus, if the guilt of Mary supplies the necessary harmonizing circumstances to render the existence of such letters conceivable or probable, there also remain sufficiently strong motives and harmonizing circumstances to render the forgery conceivable. A forgery in such circumstances would undoubtedly have been specially dangerous—dangerous to the Regent Moray in Scotland should it by any possibility have been discovered, probably still more dangerous to him should Elizabeth or her advisers have detected it, and dangerous to Elizabeth's reputation should she wittingly or unwittingly have permitted herself to be influenced by forged documents. Nevertheless, the position of the Regent Moray would undoubtedly have been more dangerous had he been destitute of the peculiarly direct and unanswerable evidence which the Casket Documents supplied. Thus, if antecedent probabilities are rather in favour of the genuineness of the letters, there is nevertheless a considerable amount of presumptive evidence to favour the conclusion that they are forgeries.

CHAPTER II.

THE PRODUCTION OF THE LETTERS IN SCOTLAND.

THE explosion at Kirk-o'-Field took place about two o'clock in the morning of the 10th February 1567. Bothwell, who was the first to inform the Queen of the occurrence, and who also later in the morning informed her of Darnley's death, was indicted for the murder, and, after a trial notoriously and palpably delusive, was formally acquitted on the 12th April. That he should have consented to a verdict of acquittal after so perfunctory an inquiry, was necessarily regarded as in itself convincing proof of his guilt. He continued to retain his position as the most confidential counsellor of the Queen, but nevertheless carried her off to Dunbar, ostensibly against her will, on the 24th April. She declined deliverance from her supposed thraldom, formally pardoned him for the abduction on the 12th May, created him Duke of Orkney, and on the 15th gave him her hand in marriage. On the 14th June she surrendered to the Lords at Carberry Hill without a blow being struck in her defence, and Bothwell, in accordance with an agreement to allow him to escape unmolested, proceeded to his stronghold of Dunbar, the Queen, in violation of the letter of the agreement, being brought a prisoner to Edinburgh, and sent on the 16th to Lochleven.

According to the declaration of Morton, made and subscribed at Westminster in December 1568, the famous silver casket containing the letters asserted to have been written by Mary to Bothwell, and other incriminating documents, came into his possession on the 20th June, or within six days of the Queen's surrender. The exact tenor of Morton's declaration has hitherto remained unknown. The name of the messenger on whom the casket was found, and the date of its discovery, were published by Buchanan; but the circumstances in which it was found, and in which its contents were produced, —vitally as they affect the whole question,—have never hitherto been published. There was, of course, the possibility that Morton's declaration would contain little new information; but it is rather curious that the special significance and importance of the declaration[1] should not have been even surmised by historians. Before considering its statements, it is, however, necessary to make a rapid survey of the history of the letters, and of the chief phases of the prolonged controversy to which they have given rise—a controversy marked by many alternations and full of strange surprises.

There is a possible reference to the Casket Docu-

[1] See Appendix A, p. 113.

ments in an Act of the Scottish Privy Council of 26th June,—six days after the date given for the discovery of the casket,—in which the Lords state that they have evident proof "as well of witnesses as of writings" that Bothwell was the principal deviser of Darnley's murder, but the reference is perhaps too vague to be regarded as more than faintly corroborative. The only writings compromising Bothwell now known to have existed are the Casket Documents, and the supposed bond for Darnley's murder, which may or may not have been a casket document; but, as other now unknown writings compromising him may then have been in existence, it cannot be asserted, apart from other evidence, that the reference is inevitably to the writings found in the casket.

A statement of Throckmorton in a letter to Cecil of the 25th July is much more definite. He mentions the intention of the Lords to charge Mary with the murder "from the testimony of her own handwriting." True, he does not actually state that the handwriting is in the form of letters, far less of letters to Bothwell; but, as a matter of fact, no other handwriting of Mary's, except that of the documents in the casket, ever was produced against her. The special significance of Throckmorton's statement is that it seems to show that, had Mary not consented to sign at Lochleven her resignation of the crown, the Lords were prepared to put her on trial for the murder, adducing her own handwriting as the principal evidence against her. Did they threaten Mary with the production of the Casket Documents when they induced her to sign her resignation? If they did not, then probably the documents were a forgery; if they did, the presumption is that they were genuine. In consenting to her resignation when threatened with a trial, she compromised herself almost as fatally as she did in marrying Bothwell. Her best friends were hard put to it to frame even plausible excuses for her conduct. Thus her secretary, Claude Nau, in his *History of Mary Stuart*,[1] asserts not merely that her life was in immediate danger—as, no doubt, would be the case if the Casket Documents were genuine; and that Lindsay informed her that she would compel them to cut her throat—as he probably did; but also that it was the intention of the "rebels" either to throw her into the lake in crossing it, or to convey her secretly to some island in the middle of the sea, there to be kept unknown to the whole world. For this wild and improbable story he does not profess to have any other evidence than that Lindsay asserted that if she did not subscribe, he had charge to "carry her to a place where he would give a good account of her to the Lords of the country." These excuses are prefaced by a very remarkable disclosure which may possibly have been communicated to him by Mary: "that she was then lying in her bed in a state of

[1] Published with Historical Preface by the Rev. Joseph Stevenson, S.J., in 1883.

very great weakness, partly by reason of her extreme trouble, partly by reason of a great flux (the result of a miscarriage of twins, her issue by Bothwell), so that she could move only with great difficulty." Father Stevenson thinks it by no means "incredible that the birth of these children was never known to the Laird of Lochleven." But the excuses of Nau, whether they rest on fact or not, are somewhat discounted by the firm attitude which he represents the Queen as assuming. He also further affirms that she frequently called those present to witness that she would observe the instruments no longer than during her imprisonment, a threat which would furnish a sufficient reason for making that imprisonment perpetual.[1] The balance of probability seems, therefore, decidedly to lean towards the conclusion, that Mary at Lochleven was informed of the discovery of the Casket Documents, although the probability falls several degrees short of certainty.

A letter of De Silva to Philip II. of Spain, on the 2nd August following, has been printed by Mr. Froude in his *History of England* as irrefragable proof of the existence of the Casket Documents soon after the assigned date of their discovery. From the information of Moray, then in London on his way from France to Scotland, De Silva gives a description of a letter of the Queen of Scots, which Mr. Froude identifies with the famous Letter 2 from Glasgow. The reply to this has been that in several important

[1] Mary instructed her Commissioners to make a similar statement.

respects the description does not tally with the character of the letter subsequently produced; much being made especially of De Silva's statement that the blowing up of the house with gunpowder was referred to in the letter. This was certainly not directly alluded to in Letter 2. On account of these discrepancies, Mr. Hosack had no difficulty in at once inferring that the letter could then have been only in the process of fabrication, and that its tenor was afterwards materially altered. This is undoubtedly making too much of the matter. Discrepancies are almost inevitable in descriptions at second or third hand, and instances of a much more extreme kind are constantly met with. At the same time, had De Silva's statement been absolutely accurate as a description of the letter, his reference would, of course, have had more weight than can be now assigned to it. Its inaccuracy so detracts from its force that it cannot be regarded as in itself a very conclusive proof, and only acquires importance as harmonizing with other corroborative evidence.

The next reference to the discovery of the documents is in a letter from Drury to Cecil, November 28th: "The writings which did comprehend the names and consents of the chiefs for the murdering of the King are turned to ashes; the same that concerns the Queen's part kept to be shewn." The statement of Drury as to the burning of the supposed bond for Darnley's murder—usually referred to as the Craigmillar bond—may be taken for what it is worth. Mr. Froude, accepting the statement of Drury, remarks, "To have permitted it" (the destruction of the bond), "may pass for a blot on Murray's escutcheon, if the paper was ever in his hands; more probably it was never allowed to reach his eyes."[1] Drury, doubtless, repeated nothing more than current speculation, for it was not likely that those who burned the bond would inform him or any one else that they had done so. Lord Herries asserted that the silver casket—the discovery of which he did not deny—never contained anything else than bonds between Bothwell and the Lords who now accused Bothwell and the Queen.[2] James Ormiston confessed on the scaffold that Bothwell had shown him a bond as a warrant for Darnley's murder, and that it was subscribed by Huntly, Argyll, Maitland, and Balfour. The weight of evidence is, however, against the supposition that this bond ever was in the casket at all. According to one account, it was left in the keeping of Argyll; Claude Nau, again, asserts, apparently on Mary's authority, that Bothwell delivered the bond to her before parting with her at Carberry Hill; and there is still a third version: "This bond was kept in the castle in a little box covered with green cloth, and after the apprehension of the Scottish Queen at Carberry Hill was taken out of the place where it lay by the Laird of Lethington, in presence of Mr.

---

[1] *History of England*, Cab. ed. viii. 295.
[2] *Memoirs of Marie Queen of Scots* (*Abbotsford Club*), p. 95.

James Balfour, the clerk of the register and keeper of the keys where the registers are." [1] Leaving this question out of account, the statement of Drury supplies no information of very special moment, except in regard to the intentions of the Lords to show the letters. It renders it, apart from other considerations, highly probable that they were shown either at the meeting of the Confederate Nobles held on the 4th December following, or at the meeting of Parliament held on the 15th, or at both meetings. In the minute of the former meeting they are, however, described as "written and subscrivit with her awen hand," while in the Act of Parliament they are described as "hailly written with her awen hand," the word "subscrivit" being omitted. As the letters finally produced at Westminster do not appear to have been subscribed by Mary, though certain contracts were, the supposed inaccuracy in the minute of the meeting of the Confederates has been regarded by some as strong presumptive evidence that the letters were not shown at either meeting: were not, in fact, produced in Scotland at all, and did not then exist in the final form in which they were subsequently produced at Westminster. Even, however, were the premises granted, such a method of reasoning would be suicidal; for if the fact that they were inaccurately described in the minute of the Confederate Nobles' meeting must be regarded

[1] Randolph to Cecil, 15th October 1570, in *Cal. State Papers*, For. Ser. 1569-71, entry 1334.

as establishing that they were not shown at that meeting, the fact that they are accurately described in the Act of Parliament must be regarded as presumptive proof that they were produced at the meeting of Parliament. Another theory which has been propounded in all seriousness, even by such a historical authority as Professor Schiern, is that in the case of some of the letters—really subscribed by Mary, but addressed to Darnley—the subscription and address were removed between the meeting of the Lords on the 4th and the meeting of the Estates on the 15th December! Plainly, it is possible to make too much of such an inaccuracy even had it existed; but the probability is that, except as regards the possibly accidental substitution of "and" for "or" between "written" and "subscrivit," the whole matter is a mare's nest. In the declaration of the Regent Moray and others regarding the authenticity of the documents, they are referred to thus: "We haif producit divers missive letteris, sonnettis, obligatiounis or contractis for marriage betwix the Quene, moder to our said Soverane, and James sometime Erle Bothwille *as writtin or subscrivit be hir hand.*"[1] Moreover, according to the usage of that time in Scotland, "letters" was a general name for all kinds of written documents, "missive letters" being the special and distinctive name for what are now usually called letters. Thus the Casket Documents are described in the

[1] Goodall, ii. 92.

following manner in the receipt of Morton, 22nd January 1570-71: "the missive letteris, contractis, or obligatiounis for marriage, sonettis, or luif-balettis *and utheris letteris* thairin contenit, to the number of XXI., send and past betwix the Quene, our said Soverane Lordis moder, and James sumtime Erle Bothville." We have only, therefore, to suppose that in the minute of the Confederate Lords' meeting the whole of the documents were comprehensively described under the term "letters," and that in the Act of Parliament the principal reference was to the "missive letters," and the supposed contradiction disappears.

A still stronger objection has, however, been mooted in the small posthumous volume of Hosack, in defence of Mary Queen of Scots, published in 1888; and the objection has been accepted by many as both well founded and, as regards the genuineness of the letters, formidable, if not fatal. Happening to discover—what, however, has been sufficiently well known since the publication of vol. i. of the *Register of the Privy Council of Scotland* in 1877—that the minute of the Confederate Nobles' meeting was not contained in the Council Book in the Register Office, Hosack announced it as an "inevitable conclusion" that the Act was a forgery, and that the Regent Moray and his associates, in forwarding it to Cecil, were guilty of "practising imposition" upon "the English government, by pretending to furnish a

[1] Goodall, ii. 91.

judicial declaration of the Queen's guilt." Even if there be some force in this objection, much of its effectiveness is lost by over-statement, for the conclusion at which Hosack arrives is certainly not an "inevitable" one; it is even at the best only possible, and very many other considerations would be required to render it so much as probable. It may also be remarked *in limine* that, if the conclusion were accepted, it would dispose of the objection that has been taken to "written and subscrivit;" for the minute was not sent to Cecil till 1568, consequently subsequent to the meeting of the Scottish Parliament; and when it was sent, the forgers, if they were forgers, had decided that the letters which they affirmed to be written by Mary were not to be produced in a subscribed form. Passing from this, the conclusion of Hosack could in any case only be accepted on the supposition that no plausible reasons could be adduced why the Privy Council should, while passing such an Act and retaining a copy of it, nevertheless have deemed it inexpedient, or even unfair to the Queen,—before her escape from Lochleven,—to have entered it in the Council Book. The true explanation, or at least a sufficient explanation, however, is that Hosack allowed himself to be deluded by a mere title. Though the minute is headed an "Act of the Secret Council" in the State Papers, the meeting is not represented in the body of the minute as a meeting merely of the Secret Council. On the contrary, the first sentence of the minute begins thus: "The which daie my Lord Regentis grace, the Lordes of Secret Counsale, and *utheris, barons and men of jugement* above written, being convenit in counsale;" and the signatures attached to the minute, which number thirty names in all, attest the accuracy of this description. In the words of Martin Philippson, published a few months before the volume of Hosack saw the light: "les titles que les membres de l'assemblée du 4 de décembre se décernent à ceux-mêmes prouvent suffisament qu'il ne peut pas être question d'un corps officiel."[1] The theory that the minute was forged is moreover entirely disposed of by the consideration that the Regent could not have ventured to bring the question of the Casket Letters before Parliament until it had been fully discussed either by the Secret Council, or by the members of such an assembly as that described in the minute. According to the minute, it was discussed at great length and upon "sundry days;" but no means could be found to obtain a "full and perfect law and securitie" except "be oppynynge and reveling of the trewth and grund of the haill matter fra the beginninge plainlie and uprichtlie, quhilk (in sa far as the manifestation thereof maie tend to the dishonor or disestimation of the Quene) they air most loith to entre in."[2]

It is not stated whether the Casket Documents were read to the assembly, or whether the repre-

[1] *Revue Historique*, xxxiv. 229.
[2] Goodall, ii. 63.

sentations of the Regent and Privy Council were taken on trust. In like manner no mention is made in the Act of Parliament of the documents having been read. The question as to whether they were read in Parliament is a matter of some importance. It has even been argued that, if they were read without the question of forgery being raised, their genuineness must be regarded as conclusively established. Both Hill Burton and Mr. Froude have laid special stress on the fact that Huntly and others did not protest against the truth of the charges, but only "against an Act that was prejudicial to the honour, power, and state of the Queen." Mr. Froude also adds: "Lord Huntly was repeatedly mentioned in them, with details of his conduct which could have been known to no one but himself and the Queen; and had no such conversations taken place as the Queen described, no one could have contradicted them more easily."[1] The silence of Huntly is undoubtedly suspicious, but it is by no means conclusive of the genuineness of the letters. In any case, he was involved in the plot against Darnley; and fear lest an accusation should have been raised against him might for the time have kept him silent. Moreover, there is the possibility that he had informed Maitland or others of his conversations with the Queen; or the forgers might have made use of intelligence obtained through some private writings of Mary. Chalmers asserts that the letters were not

[1] *History of England*, Cab. ed. viii. 299.

laid before Parliament, and Mr. Skelton thinks they were only "tabled *pro forma* with the Act;" but it is difficult to understand how either of these propositions can be maintained in view of the declaration of the Queen's nobles convened at Dumbarton, 12th September 1568 : "And gif it beis alledgit, that hir Majestie's writing, producit in parliament, sould preive her grace culpabill, it may be answerit, That there is in na place mentioun maid in it, be the quhilk hir Hienes may be convict, albeit it were hir awin hand-writ, as it is not. And also the samin is devysit be thameselfis in sum principal and substantious clausis."[1] This statement clearly shows, not only that the letters were produced, but that they were read. At the same time, the nobles were so far justified in declaring that "quhat was done, it was not to declair hir grace guiltie of ony crime, quhilk of ressoun na wayis could be done contrare hir Majestie uncallit, but onlie ane act maid for safetie of thameselves fra foirfaltour." The Queen's friends at the Parliament contented themselves with a somewhat ambiguous protest, while the other party contented themselves with passing a somewhat illogical and contradictory Act. The whole tendency of the evidence now adduced is, however, to favour the supposition that the Casket Letters were genuine. There is nothing in the procedure of the Lords of such a character as necessarily to afford ground for doubt or suspicion

[1] Goodall, ii. 361

of their genuineness, while there is much in the conduct of the Queen and her supporters to indicate that they dreaded their production. At the same time, though the balance of the evidence, so far as it has been now considered, is in favour of the letters, without further corroboration it cannot be termed overwhelming or irrefragable.

CHAPTER III.

THE PRODUCTION OF THE LETTERS IN ENGLAND.

QUEEN MARY made her escape from Lochleven on the 2nd May 1568, but, being defeated at Langside on the 13th, galloped with a few followers to the Borders, and on the 16th crossed the Solway in a fishing-boat to Workington in Cumberland. Her pathetic and well-argued appeals to the womanly consideration and regal fellow-feeling of Elizabeth constrained the Regent Moray to transmit to the English Queen a counteractive. Accordingly, on the 22nd June he informed Mr. Middlemore that he had sent with Mr. John Wood the letters of Mary to Bothwell, " translated into our language, to be considered by the judges that shall have examination and commission of the matter." His special object in sending the translations was stated to be that the judges " may resolve us thus far, in case the principal agree with the copy, that then we prove the cause indeed; for when we have manifested and shown all, and yet shall have no assurance that it we send shall satisfy for probation, for what purpose shall we either accuse, or take care how to prove, when we are not assured what to prove, or when we have proved what shall succeed?"[1] For the wariness he here manifests Moray had sufficient cause. He had already had unpleasant experience of Elizabeth's capricious temper and uncertain policy; for, on presenting himself at Court in 1565, after having done his best at her instigation to oppose the Darnley marriage, he had been ignominiously dismissed as an "unworthy traitor" to his sovereign. Moreover, Elizabeth had all along decidedly opposed the imprisonment of Mary in Lochleven.

In reply to Moray's communication, Elizabeth desired him to send some persons of good quality to Newcastle or Durham, to treat of the "great matter of the Queen of Scots;" and requested also that the meeting of the Scottish Parliament appointed to be held in August might be meantime suspended.[2] Moray found himself unable to agree to the proposal to defer the meeting of the Parliament, but he nevertheless, in deference to her requests, suspended some of the proceedings of forfeiture, and shortly afterwards a conference was appointed to be held at York in the last week of October.

It would widen too much the scope of the present inquiry to endeavour to determine how far the procedure of Elizabeth and Moray towards the Queen of Scots was legally justifiable, or in other respects entirely fair and equitable. The whole of the pro-

---

[1] Letter printed in Goodall, ii. 76.
[2] *Calendar Scottish State Papers*, i. 264.

cedure was indeed, from a strictly legal point of view, irregular, as procedure against sovereigns must almost necessarily be. So far as the Scottish Commission were concerned, it is to be borne in mind that they never acknowledged the English Commissioners as in any sense a tribunal. They were merely engaged in conference with the commissioners of a friendly power, whose alliance and friendship they desired to maintain, and to whom their deposed sovereign was appealing, not only for protection, but for aid to restore her to her throne. The primary object of the conference was to bring about a *modus vivendi*, not only as between Elizabeth and the Confederate Lords of Scotland, but, if possible, between the Queen of Scots and them. There is no information as to whether Wood, before the meeting of the Commissioners at York, had shown the letters to any one, but, as he was only authorized to show them to commissioners specially appointed to consider them, the probability is that they were not shown. The Scottish Commissioners carried with them to York the silver casket with the original documents, and, previous to setting out from Edinburgh, the Regent Moray, on 16th September, "taking the burden upon him for the remanent noblemen and others," gave a receipt to the Privy Council for the casket, which had been in the keeping of Morton. In the receipt he testified that Morton had "trewlie and honestlie observit and kepit the said box and haill writtis and pecis foirsaidis within the same, without ony alteratioun, augmentatioun, or diminutioun tharcof in ony part or portioun;" and promised that "saidis haill lettres and writtingis salbe alwayis readie and furtheumand to the said Erll of Mortoun and remanent nobill men that enterit in the querrell of revengeing of the King our Soverane Lordis faderis murthour, quhensoevir thai sal haif to do thairwith, for manifesting of the ground and equitie of thair procedingis to all quhome it efferis."[1] Still anxious not to commit himself to a public accusation of the Queen of Scots before he had some assurance as to how Elizabeth "would judge of the matter," Moray deputed Maitland of Lethington, James Makgill, George Buchanan, and John Wood to show the letters privately to the English Commissioners, in order that they might unofficially communicate their contents to Elizabeth. This procedure was irregular, and has been severely condemned by the defenders of the Scottish Queen, but it can scarcely be affirmed either that she suffered from it any substantial injustice, or that on Moray's part it indicated any disbelief in the genuineness of the letters. It might or might not indicate that he was afraid of the possible counter-accusations that might be brought against some of his colleagues; but to prove the truth of these accusations does not tend to disprove the genuineness of the letters. In considering the bearing of his conduct on the genuineness of the letters, it is sufficient to point out that he was

[1] *Register of the Privy Council of Scotland*, i. 641.

perfectly justified in hesitating to commit himself to an irretrievable course of action, before he had some assurance that Elizabeth would be guided in her decision by the evidence he had to adduce. All that he wished to know was whether, on the supposition that the letters were proved to be genuine, Elizabeth would admit them to be conclusive evidence against the Queen of Scots. There were also reasons why he should give her fair warning of the extraordinary character of the evidence he had in his possession. She had stated in July to the Spanish Ambassador that the letters were a forgery; probably she had also indirectly hinted to Moray that she entertained grave doubts on the subject; and by the step he took he at least gave her to know that he was determined to take his stand upon their genuineness.

From the fact that the "principal points" of the letters sent by the English Commissioners to Elizabeth were in Scots, it has been assumed by Hosack, Mr. Skelton, and others, that only the Scottish version was shown at York to the English Commissioners. The assumption is made in order to give support to the extraordinary theory that they actually exhibited the Scottish letters as the originals. The Commissioners state that "theis men here do constantly affirme the said lres and other writings wch they produce of her owne hand, to be of her own hande in dede;" and they also referred to them as "closed in a little coffer of silver and gilte, hertofore geaven by her to Bothwill." Plainly, therefore, if they took the Scottish letters out of the silver casket, and asserted them to have been written by Mary's "own hand," there can be no doubt whatever that the French letters afterwards exhibited at Westminster were forgeries. The question might thus be regarded as disposed of once and for all. But while the assumption has been made on the narrowest grounds, and, in fact, without evidence of a more substantial kind than mere superficial possibility, the following difficulties must be surmounted before it can be regarded with seriousness. It must be explained why the Regent Moray stated in the letter of the 22nd June that the Scottish version was merely a translation; why the Scottish Privy Council agreed, on Moray's return to Scotland, to accept as genuine French versions, when they knew, if the supposition of Hosack is to be accepted, that the versions he had carried with him into England were in Scots; why Moray, after taking care to have the letters forged in the Queen's hand in Scots for the York Conference, should have thought it necessary or wise, when the *venue* was changed to London, to exhibit them forged in the Queen's hand in French; and why it never struck the English Commissioners that, since he had exhibited the Scots version at York as the original one, he was somewhat straining their credulity by exhibiting at London the French versions as the original.

When so much has been disputed about the letters, there is some satisfaction in being able to state that all parties are agreed that the French version was exhibited at Westminster, to which the Conference adjourned in December, and that it was exhibited as the original version. The records of the Conference supply a list of the incriminating Casket Documents exhibited at the Conference, and it is as follows:[1] 1st, A promise (in French) by Mary of marriage to Bothwell, without date; 2nd, a marriage contract in Scots, asserted to be in the handwriting of the Earl of Huntly, professedly subscribed by Mary and Bothwell, and dated, at Seton, 5th April, seven days before Bothwell's acquittal of the murder, and nineteen days before Mary was brought, whether willingly or unwillingly, by Bothwell to Dunbar; and 3rd, nine letters (in French) of Mary to Bothwell, including the French poem usually referred to as the sonnet, but incorrectly so, for even its separate stanzas are not in strict sonnet form. The only letters in themselves of an absolutely compromising kind are the Glasgow letters,—Nos. 1 and 2,—which, if genuine, prove that Mary was the agent of Bothwell in enticing Darnley to his doom; and Nos. 6, 7, and 8, written some or all of them from Stirling, and demonstrating, if genuine, that Mary was herself the instigator of her colourable capture by Bothwell, and confinement in Dunbar. Letters 3, 4, and 5, read in the light of the others, and on the supposition that they were sent to Bothwell, are distinctly compromising; but in themselves, and apart from the person to whom

[1] See Appendix C, p. 121.

they may have been addressed, contain nothing, or almost nothing, inconsistent with the innocence of the writer.

In the records of the Commission it is not stated whether or not the Scottish Commission exhibited at Westminster all the documents in the casket. Before they were read, Morton produced the declaration in regard to the time and manner in which the casket came into his possession. The Scottish Commissioners, Moray, Morton, Bothwell bishop of Orkney, Lord Lindsay, and Pitcairn commendator of Dunfermline, also made a declaration, to the effect that "the saidis haill missive writingis, sonettis, and obligatiounis or contractis, are undoubtedly the said Quenis proper hand-write; except the contract in Scottis, of the dait, at Seitoun, the fift day of Aprile 1567, written be the Erle of Huntly, quhilk alsua we understand and perfectlie knawis to be subscrivit be hir, and will tak the same upon our honours and consciences, as is befoir said."[1] Copies were made of all the documents in the original language in which they were written; and, in order that the meaning might be more fully understood by all the Commissioners, the letters were also translated into English. After the taking of the evidence was concluded, some of the chief nobility were summoned to meet the Privy Council on the 14th December. The meeting was continued to the 15th, and the whole of the evidence taken was read over and considered.

[1] Goodall, ii. 92.

The noblemen summoned to the meeting included the Catholic Earls of Norfolk, Westmoreland, and Northumberland, and others who, in the words of Mr. Froude, had "made themselves most conspicuous as the advocates of the Queen of Scots." After a narrative had been given of the proceedings at Westminster, "there were produced sundry letters in French, supposed to be written by the Queene of Scots own hand, to the Erle Bothwell; and therewith also one long sonnet; and a promise of marriage in the name of the said Quene with the said Erle Bothwell. Of which lettres the originals, supposed to be written with the Quene of Scotts own hand, were then also presently produced and perused; and, being read, were duly conferred and compared, for the manner of writing and fashion of orthography, with sundry other lettres long since heretofore written, and sent by the said Quene of Scotts to the Quene's Majesty. And next after these was produced and read a declaration of the Erle Morton, of the manner of the finding of the said lettres, as the same was exhibited upon his oath the 9th of December: In collation whereof no difference was found. Of all which lettres and writings the true copies are contained in the memorial of the acts of the sessions of the 7th and 8th December."[1]

After quoting this minute of the 14th December, Hosack proceeds as follows: "It is important to ascertain in what way this examination was made,

---

[1] See Appendix D, p. 188.

and it is described in the following graphic terms by Cecil himself: 'It is to be noted that at the time of the producing, showing, and reading of all these foresaid writings there was no special choice nor regard had to the order of the producing thereof; but the whole writings lying altogether upon the council table, the same were one after another showed rather by hap as the same did lie on the table, than with any choice made, as by the natures thereof, if time had so served, might have been.' What is meant by the expression 'if time had so served' we can only guess; and it is remarkable that the Secretary, usually so calm, patient, and methodical, should have allowed an investigation of this kind to be conducted in the confused and hurried manner he has himself described. When we consider that the whole question depended on the genuineness of these letters, the bitterest enemy of the Scottish Queen will hardly maintain that this kind of haphazard inspection in the absence of the accused, or of any one on her behalf, was satisfactory."[1] These comments of Hosack have been adopted and specially emphasized by subsequent writers in defence of the Queen, even by Professor Schiern, of Copenhagen, in his *Life of Bothwell*, and by Mr. Skelton, both in his essay on the "Impeachment of Mary Queen of Scots," republished in 1876, and in vol. ii. of *Maitland of Lethington*, published in 1888. Mr. Skelton, to aid the reader to discern more clearly the character of Cecil's

[1] *Mary Queen of Scots and her Accusers* (1869), i. 449.

delinquency, has taken the trouble to print the specially damaging passages of what he sarcastically terms Cecil's "frank admission" in italics, thus: "there was *no special choice nor regard had to the order of the producing thereof;*" and "*if time had so served.*" With appropriate indignation he also remarks: "Why this vitally important examination should have been delayed till the last moment, and why, when it did take place, it should have been hurried over, are facts which have not been explained."[1] It seems, indeed, quite manifest that both Hosack and Mr. Skelton, with their special legal training and experience, are genuinely surprised at the unblushing and explicit frankness of Cecil in confessing, or rather ingenuously recording, his striking and criminal carelessness in regard to the comparison of the letters. The language Cecil employs is indeed rather puzzling; and Hosack was constrained to observe: "What was meant by the expression 'if time had so served' we can only guess." He guessed, however, that the language concealed something very bad indeed; and all three, Hosack, Professor Schiern, and Mr. Skelton, were necessarily at one in agreeing that the method of procedure, in reference to the letters, thus described by Cecil, was in the highest degree suspicious, and almost conclusive proof that he was acting in collusion with the Scottish Commissioners to pass off forged letters for genuine ones. The chief difficulty in accepting their conclusion is

[1] *Maitland of Lethington*, ii. 319.

that the carelessness, if it be chargeable against any persons, is chargeable against Hosack, Professor Schiern, and Mr. Skelton rather than against Cecil. It is certainly remarkable that three independent inquirers of such eminence and ability should unwittingly have united in giving currency to such a total misrepresentation of Cecil's procedure. The original promulgator of the extraordinary mistake appears to have been Hosack—though possibly he may have borrowed it from some previous writer; but why, in a matter so vitally affecting the genuineness of the letters, he, all the time admitting that Cecil's conduct in this instance was strange and unusual, should have allowed himself to fall into such a plain and palpable error, and why Professor Schiern and Mr. Skelton should have blindly followed in his footsteps without any suspicion that they were going fatally astray, is certainly very difficult to explain. To enable Hosack to arrive at the conclusion which caused him such genuine astonishment, it was necessary to roll two days into one. Cecil's words, "It is to be noted," etc., have not the smallest reference to the procedure on the 14th December, when the Casket Letters were examined, but refer *solely and entirely* to the papers read and considered on the 15th December. They do not occur in the minute of the 14th, but in the minute of the 15th. On the 14th the letters "were duly conferred and compared," after which Morton's declaration; the examination of certain persons who had been executed for the murder; and the confession and deposition of Thomas Crawford were read. And "as the night approached," the "further declaration of the rest" was deferred till the following day. On that day a "great length of time," as is stated, was spent in the reading of other "sundry kinds of writings," and it is solely in regard to the "producing, showing, and reading" of these writings, that, according to the minute, there was "no special choice nor regard had to the order of the producing thereof, but the whole writings lying altogether upon the council table, the same were one after another showed rather by hap," etc.[1] Even apart from the unmistakeable character of the reference in the minute, it is absurd to suppose that the Casket Letters were tumbled out on the council table, where they lay along with the other papers, and were examined at haphazard. The words of the minute of the 15th are thus essentially inapplicable to the letters in the casket. The only bearing this minute has on the question of their authenticity is to show how conscientiously and carefully the procedure of the Commission is described in the minutes, and to lend additional weight to the statement in the minute of the 14th in regard to the comparison of the Casket Letters, both "for the manner of writing and fashion of orthography," with other genuine letters of the Queen. The whole weight of evidence goes to show that, if the docu-

---

[1] See "Journal of Proceedings" of the Commissioners at Hampton Court—Appendix D, p. 186.

ments were forgeries, the Regent Moray and his colleagues succeeded in entirely deceiving both Cecil and the other English Commissioners, and deceiving them after an exhaustive examination of the letters, and a minute and detailed comparison of them with genuine writings of the Queen of Scots. The reason why this comparison was deferred — it was not deferred to the "last moment"—was in order that those English earls who were known to favour Mary's cause might be present when it took place. Had the examination taken place previously, it might have been said that the matter had been decided before their opinion was asked. It is true the Commissioners of Mary were not present, but they had declined to attend. Whether their reasons were satisfactory or not, is a disputed point; but it cannot be affirmed, since the examination took place in the presence of the Catholic lords, that "no one was present on her behalf."

The Scottish Commissioners brought the casket with its contents to Scotland, and it was placed in charge of the Regent. It was again entrusted to Morton in January 1570-71, when he set out on an embassy to London. In the receipt granted by Morton to the Regent Lennox, the documents are stated to number in all twenty-one. Before being entrusted to Morton, they were "autentiklie copeit, and subscrivit with the handis of his grace and Lordes of Secreit Counsale," the copies being "left to remane with his grace *ad futuram rei memoriam.*" Morton at the same time came under an obligation to bring the casket and documents with him on his return, as he had received them; and he did so. After Morton's execution, they were delivered by his natural son, James, Prior of Pluscardin, to the Earl of Gowrie, who declined, notwithstanding the repeated entreaties of Bowes, the English Ambassador, to deliver them up to Elizabeth.

CHAPTER IV.

THE PUBLICATION OF THE LETTERS.

THE previous chapter contains a brief summary of all that for two centuries was known regarding the origin and history of these famous documents. Not only the alleged original letters of Mary, but the missing French copies, certain English translations that were made at Westminster, and the original copies of the Scottish translations, disappeared completely from human ken. This was partly, but not wholly, to be accounted for by the difficult conditions under which at one time research could be prosecuted for original documents in public and private archives. A succinct summary of their contents, with quotations in Scots, was published in the *Sadler Correspondence*, but, had not translations of them been appended to the editions of Buchanan's *Detection*, a full acquaintance with their statements would during all these years have been impossible. We learn from the *Bowes Correspondence* that Esme Stewart, Duke of Lennox, the secret representative of the Catholics, was as anxious as Elizabeth to obtain possession of the originals, but in this he probably did not succeed.

The likelihood is that, after the execution of the Earl of Gowrie, at the instance of James Stewart, Earl of Arran, then the favourite of James VI., they passed into Arran's hands. In any case, the statements in the *Bowes Correspondence* refute the supposition of Walter Goodall that after the execution of Morton the box and letters passed into the hands of the Earl of Angus and his successors. Goodall's reason for the statement is that an anonymous historian, who " wrote about the restoration of King Charles II.," affirmed that the box and writings were at that time to be seen with the Marquis of Douglas. He adds, " It is thought by some that they were still in that family, though others say they have since been seen at Hamilton." [1] Goodall, who wrote in 1754, here labours under some confusion, owing to defective genealogical knowledge. William, third Duke of Hamilton, who died in 1694, consequently before Goodall wrote, was the eldest son of the first Marquis of Douglas. He married Anne, Duchess of Hamilton, daughter of the first duke, and thus came into possession of the Hamilton estates. Therefore, had the casket been in the possession of the Marquis of Douglas, it might have been brought by the third duke to Hamilton. Probably, however, it never came into the possession of the Marquis of Douglas; but if it came into the possession of the Hamiltons, this is sufficiently accounted for by the fact that Arran was for some time in possession of the

[1] Goodall, i. 36.

Hamilton estates. A silver casket, of the size of the Bothwell one, and marked in two places with the letter F, is now at Hamilton Palace. The gilding and other ornaments are, however, absent, and thus in any case the evidence is not complete for its absolute identification. Gabriel Naudé—who professed his willingness to believe "all that Monsieurs de Thou and Buchanan said to be very true"—asserted that he had seen the letters at Rome, but whether those he saw were originals or only copies is not stated. The copy of the documents made at the instance of the Regent Lennox and the Privy Council in January 1570-71, and probably contained in the Register of the Council, has disappeared; but this is sufficiently accounted for by the fact that the whole of the register during the period of the regency of Lennox has been destroyed. The Act of Parliament of the 15th December was also expunged from the official records; and only the accident of its having been printed in 1568 has preserved to us its reference to the Casket Documents. Certain copies, afterwards to be referred to, of the letters have been preserved in the Record Office and at Hatfield, but have only been discovered within recent years.

If the total disappearance of the original Casket Documents, the disappearance even of the copies of some of the most important of them, and the expunging of the references to them from the official records of Scotland, have any significance at all, these facts go to support the conclusion that they were genuine rather than the conclusion that they were forgeries. It is clear that they were not destroyed by the party who are asserted to have forged them. That party, on the contrary, used the utmost precautions to preserve them, as the most complete vindication possible of their conduct towards the Queen; and in order that an exact record of their language might be preserved—even if the originals should be lost—caused them to be copied in the original French, and attested by the signatures of the Privy Council. In entire consistency with this attitude, the Earl of Gowrie replied to Elizabeth's requests for the deliverance of the letters to her, that "he could not deliver them to any person without the consents and privities as well of the King, that had interest therein, as also of the rest of the noblemen enterprisers of the action against the King's mother, and that would have them kept as an evidence to warrant and make good that action."[1] Elizabeth's anxiety to have them in her possession, or rather to prevent them falling into the hands of the friends of the Queen of Scots, is quite consistent with her belief in their genuineness. Her principal excuse for keeping the Queen of Scots in England was that she had been guilty of the murder. Notwithstanding any other statements to the contrary, it was understood between her and the Scottish Commissioners that Mary's guilt had been established by the letters. Should the letters be destroyed,

---

[1] *Bowes Correspondence* (Surtees Society), p. 241.

Elizabeth recognised that she would be left without a tangible justification in supporting the action of the Scottish nobles against their sovereign. On the other hand, if, after Gowrie's execution, they really fell into the hands of the Marian party, their disappearance must be regarded as a strong presumption that they were genuine; but if they fell directly into the hands of King James, and were destroyed by his orders, the matter is by no means so clear. As the conduct of the Scottish monarch towards his mother —especially his passive attitude in regard to her execution—can scarcely be termed irreproachable, he had reasons, on the supposition that the letters were forged, for not establishing too clearly that the most convincing evidence against her conduct in Scotland was false. Therefore he was unlikely to expose the forgery. But, again, he was not personally responsible either for his mother's imprisonment or her execution; an indelible stain on her reputation reflected on himself; whether the letters were genuine or not, they had already served their purpose, and naturally he would be unwilling to preserve such damning evidence of his mother's misdeeds, or even the official reference to it, when no practical advantage to himself was to be gained by doing so.

The following account of the publication of the letters in editions of Buchanan's *Detection* is given by Mr. Skelton in his picturesque and fascinating volumes on Maitland of Lethington: "They were first made public in 1571, appended to the *Detectio Mariæ Reginæ* of Buchanan, which was published in the Latin and Scots languages during that year—a French translation appearing in 1572. There is no reason to suppose that the Latin version of the *Detectio* was not revised by Buchanan as it went through the press; and there is every reason to believe that the Scots version (published by authority of Cecil) was made by Buchanan himself, as it bears constant traces of his vigorous and sinewy style, and is perhaps the most perfect specimen of the classical Scots which we possess. The French edition, in spite of some transparent mystification, stands substantially in the same position,—it was the fruit of the obscure but sleepless activity of Cecil. Most of the letters were printed in the Scots and French editions,—three only in the Latin."[1] He also refers to the French version as "thus jointly guaranteed as it were by Buchanan and Cecil." The above statements are here quoted because they present almost a travesty of the facts relating to Buchanan's *Detection;* the modicum of truth they contain being partially hidden or distorted by directly erroneous statement, unfair insinuation, or groundless inference. To the Latin version of the *Detection*, published, as is known from other evidence, at London in 1571, but under the title *De Maria Scotorum Regina*, etc., and without indicating place of publication, date, printer, or author, only three letters in Latin were appended.

[1] ii. 328.

The title was subsequently changed to *Detectio Mariæ Reginæ*, etc., and it was published under this title in Buchanan's *Opera*. In 1571 a Scots version under the title "*Ane Detection of the duinges of Marie Quene of Scottis*, etc., translated out of the Latine quhilke was written by G. B.," was published at London, but without name of place, date, or printer; and in 1572 a Scots version was also published at St. Andrews. The Scots version published in 1571 in London was somewhat anglicized in its spelling to render it suitable for English readers. There was also appended to it an exhortation beginning, "Now judge, Englishmen, if it be good to change Queens." The whole eight letters were appended to the Scots versions; and the first sentence of the original French of each of the letters was also given. Only seven letters were appended to the French translation of the *Detectio*, published with the imprimatur "Edinbourg Th. Vvaltem 1572." As it is also dated 13th February, the actual year of publication was 1573. Letter 3 was never published in a French form until it was printed in 1869 by Hosack in the first volume of his work in defence of Mary Queen of Scots. The French translation, published in 1573, was the work of a Huguenot *avocat* of Rochelle, named Cumez.[1] The "transparent mystification," which Mr. Skelton does not define in specific terms, was that, while the work was professedly

---

[1] Preface to *L'Innocence De La Tres-Illustre, Tres-Chaste et Debonnaire Princesse, Madame Marie Royne D'Escosse.*

published at Edinburgh, it was really published somewhere else. By the use of the words "transparent mystification" Mr. Skelton must, if he means anything, mean to hint that it was published in London. Hosack, on the contrary, admits that the weight of evidence is in favour of the conclusion that it was published in France, but adds that the matter is of no consequence, a view which entirely differs from that of Mr. Skelton. A "mystification" to conceal the publication of the work in France, however "transparent" it might be, would not suit Mr. Skelton's argument. But, supposing the work had been printed and published in London, it would surely have been a very stupid as well as transparent mystification to have annexed to it the imprimatur "Edinbourg." Had there been no mystification, and had the work really been printed at Edinburgh, no less than had it been printed in London, we might possibly have inferred with Mr. Skelton that the letters in their French form were not merely published directly by Cecil, but published as "the identical letters which had come from the pen of Mary Stuart." On account, however, of the very transparency of the mystification—which was then in common use in regard to surreptitious works published in France—it is impossible to hold that there was any dishonest purpose in concealing the name of the printer. The hypothesis of Mr. Skelton is, moreover, entirely superfluous, and therefore unscientific; for the existence of the published

French version of the letters is sufficiently accounted for by the statement that they were translated from a Latin version of the letters. They are not represented in the French edition as anything more than translations; but it so happened that in the other editions of the *Detection* the first sentence of each of the original French versions was given, and these sentences as they stood were adopted by the translator. It is this circumstance alone that caused the misconception so long current. To assert that the French translation of the *Detection* was the "fruit of the obscure but sleepless activity of Cecil," is to seek refuge in a phrase which is a "transparent mystification." Obscure activity, however sleepless, cannot be regarded as a guarantee of anything in particular; and therefore the obscure activity of Cecil cannot be cited as a guarantee that he supplied the French version of the letters for the French translation of the *Detection*. Much controversy would doubtless have been spared, and Buchanan would have better served the interests of future generations, had he included the original French versions in the editions of the *Detection*, both Scotch and Latin, issued in this country. But it is assuming too much to suppose that dread lest the forgery might be discovered was the reason of their non-publication; and in any case, to have published French translations of the Latin version as originals would not have been a clever method of endeavouring to avoid the supposed difficulty.

CHAPTER V.

THE CONTROVERSY.

THAT the French versions of the letters were translated from the Scots or Latin was elaborately proved by Walter Goodall in his *Examination of the Letters said to be written by Mary Queen of Scots*, published in 1754. His demonstration is thus referred to by Mr. Skelton: "But in 1754 a philological contribution to the controversy was made by Goodall, which for ingenuity and research deserves to rank alongside the works of the great critics who have exercised their wits on classical antiquity. He proved that the Scots letters were the original, and that the French had been translated from the Scots, or from the Latin. This he did mainly by showing that the Scots, so to speak, were idiomatic and proverbial, and that in the French the Scots proverbs and idioms had been slavishly and clumsily reproduced. He showed, moreover, that the grossest blunders had been made by the translators."[1] With the proviso that this language smacks somewhat of hyperbole as an estimate of Goodall's critical feat,

[1] Vol. ii. 329.

and need not be interpreted too literally as a definition of what Goodall did demonstrate, the main purport of it—that Goodall demonstrated the published French versions of the letters to be a translation—may be accepted without any qualification. Nor can the supreme importance of the point be disputed. In the preface to the original French translation, it was stated that the published French version of the letters was translated from the Latin; but this preface was not reprinted in subsequent editions, and thus some delusion prevailed. The question remains, however, as to the exact significance of the demonstration. Was its significance such as Goodall supposed it to have been, or was Goodall unconsciously contributing to establish a conclusion exactly the opposite of the one he wished to establish? Goodall regarded it —and Mr. Skelton still regards it—as a conclusive proof of the forgery. Goodall supposed, in the words of Mr. Skelton, that it "entitled him to say that as the French letters which had been produced against Mary had undoubtedly been translated from another language which she barely understood,[1] he had demonstrated that she did not write them, and that they must have been fabricated by those who produced them." This conclusion of Goodall seemed

---

[1] Mr. Skelton here refers to the Scots, which Mary in 1568 wrote with some difficulty; Goodall states that the French letters were translated from "George Buchanan's *Latin.*"—*Examination of the Letters*, p. 80.

to Hosack, writing in 1869, to be confirmed, so far as it demonstrated the forgery of the letters, by certain almost providential exceptions, which only rendered the probation of the general rule more complete. Hosack's theory was in some respects an expansion, in some respects a modification, of Goodall's; but in both respects the tendency of the alterations was supposed to be towards a more conclusive establishment of the forgery. One of the special advantages of Hosack's theory was that, if true, it supplied an exposure of the ingenious methods of the forger. The Goodall theory, with Hosack's modifications and improvements, is still trustfully accepted by Mr. Skelton, who thus naively expounds it: "But it is to be observed that while as regards those portions of the letters from which Goodall mainly derived his illustrations, no reply to him is possible, yet there are other portions of certain letters, and indeed whole letters, to which his argument does not apply. As regards certain letters or portions of letters, it has been shown that the French in which they are written is idiomatic, and that the Scotch versions have been made from the French. Now, assuming that we have in every case the letters produced at Westminster, it would appear reasonable to hold (1) that the vernacular French was not written by the person who wrote the corrupt French, and (2) that the letters in which vernacular French is mixed with corrupt French have been in some way tampered with. It has been observed, moreover, that it is the corrupt French, not the vernacular French, which contain the passages that compromise the Queen."[1]

The theory of Hosack — which, however, had previously been vaguely outlined by Miss Strickland — was suggested by the providential discovery at the Record Office of the original French version of Letter 3, which, as we have seen, had never previously appeared in a French form. The peculiarity and significance of the discovery appeared to be that this was in itself a harmless love-letter, containing nothing that could be misconstrued as even in the remotest degree referring to the occurrence at Kirk-o'-Field. The importance of the letter depended altogether upon the person to whom it was addressed. Hosack started the theory that this was a genuine production of the Queen of Scots, but addressed to Darnley. Following up the clue he supposed he had discovered, he accepted the published French version of Letter 4 as "obviously the original," his reason for doing so being that certain seemingly compromising expressions in the Scots version had almost disappeared in the Latin version, and had wholly disappeared in the French version. There was, of course, the difficulty of explaining why in the Latin version no special effort had been made to retain them, when they had been specially fabricated for the Scots version; but Hosack did not even allude to the

[1] Vol. ii. p. 331.

existence of such a difficulty. It turns out that these compromising expressions can be clearly traced from the original French version of the letter at Hatfield, the existence of which was then unknown to Hosack. At Hatfield there is also an English version of the same letter. The following are the various versions of the principal compromising phrase in the letter :—(1) Original French version at Hatfield : "Car j'enseray en pein et faites bon guet si l'oseau sortira de sa cage ou sens son per comme la tourtre demeurera seulle a se lamenter de l'absence pour court quelle soit;" (2) English translation at Hatfield : "For I shall think long, And watche well if the byrde shall fly out of his cage or w'out his make, as the turtle shall remayne alone to lament & morne for absence how short soev^r it be;" (3) published Scots version : "Mak gude watch —Gif the burd eschaip out of the caige, or without his mate. As the turtur I sall remane alone for to lament the absence, how schort yet sa ever it be;" (4) published Latin version : "Si avis evaserit è cavea, aut sine compare, velut turtur, ego remanebo sola ut lamenter absentiam tuam quamlibet brevem;" (5) published French version : "Comme l'oyseau eschappé de la cage, ou la tourtre qui est sans compagne, ainsi je demeurera seule, pour pleurer vostre absence, quelque brieve qu'elle puisse estre." The process of alteration in the various versions is thus clearly visible. That the French version at Hatfield is the version exhibited at

Westminster, is, of course, beyond reasonable doubt; and Hosack, unwittingly led astray by his supposed discovery of a palpable fraud, allowed himself, by accepting the published version as the original, to fall into a mistake so serious as practically to rob his argument of whatever cogency it might have otherwise possessed. He was in no degree staggered in his theory when, in addition to the unpublished Letter 3, he found also at the Record Office a French version of Letter 5. This version, of course, differs from the published French translated version; but it so happened that it also, like No. 3, was comparatively indefinite except in the expression of affection; and, without grappling with the difficulty of the two French versions, or apparently recognising that there was such a difficulty to be grappled with, he contented himself with stating that it was probably a genuine letter of Mary's, but "appeared to have been addressed, not to Bothwell, but to Darnley." The theory of Hosack, therefore, was that, in the casket, genuine letters—but letters really sent to Darnley—were placed alongside of forged ones, which, if genuine, could not have been addressed to any one but Bothwell. This mixture of the true and the false, Hosack accounted for as a cunning device to circumvent and lead astray the judgment of the English Commissioners.

Before even venturing to moot such a theory, it was, by the ordinary rules of evidence, almost incumbent on Hosack to have advanced some proof that

forgery. Writing to his wife, who was his constant adviser, and shared all his political secrets, he declared—*apropos* of a letter to his wife from the Queen of Scots, dated 16th July 1570—that he was assured of Mary's guilt, not only by his own "knowledge, but *by her hand writ*, the confessions of men gone to the death, and other infallible experience."

Even if the considerations now adduced be not regarded as absolutely fatal to the theory that any of the letters in the casket were written to Darnley, they render it antecedently more probable that they were written to Bothwell. Bothwell, we know, could read, write, and speak French with fluency, and, on the supposition that Mary was in love with him,—a supposition in regard to which Mr. Skelton goes so far as to admit that his "judgment remains in suspense,"—there is no inherent necessity for advancing any other theory than that they were written to him.

The proposition of Hosack, that certain letters in idiomatic French were written to Darnley, was merely a pendant or confirmation of the theory that all the compromising letters, or compromising portions of otherwise genuine letters, were not written in idiomatic French, but were translations from the Scots or Latin, and consequently forgeries. It, moreover, necessarily left unaffected the theory that all the published letters in the French version of the *Detection* were supplied by Cecil and Buchanan, and were identical with those produced at Westminster. Admit that even a single one of the translated French letters is not the version produced at Westminster, and Goodall's theory, with all the momentous inferences dependent upon it, necessarily collapses. Hosack's modification of the theory, if plausible and promising, was therefore bold, if not foolhardy. Notwithstanding the advantages that might be gained by it, the modification was not one to be adopted lightly or without strong presumption in its favour. A suspicion of lurking danger seems at last to have crossed Hosack's mind when he had to recognise the existence at the Record Office of an English translation of the famous Letter 2, which, as he stated, was not a translation from any of the three published versions — Scots, Latin, or French. He thereupon expressed himself thus: "Were there two originals of these famous letters? As the alleged originals have long since disappeared, this is a question which no one can answer. We only know that from first to last everything connected with these letters is involved in mystery and contradiction." He, however, actually printed this English version, with its variations from the Scots version, in the belief that it tended to increase the suspicions against the genuineness of the letters, and to show that even the Scots version, forged though he affirmed it to be, had been further tampered with to render it more consistent with facts subsequently discovered. From the doubts and difficulties which this convenient hypothesis did not altogether allay, he was, moreover, able to deliver himself by making a discovery, or rather a criticism, which he regarded as fatal to the genuineness of the letter. This was that the passages recording the conversations between Mary and Darnley corresponded so closely with the record of these conversations contained in a declaration of Captain Thomas Crawford, Darnley's servant—handed in at Westminster—as to show either that this portion of the letter was founded on Crawford's declaration, or that Crawford's declaration was copied or modified and improved from this portion of the letter. Hosack, besides regarding the proof of collusion as incontestable, adduced arguments, which he esteemed conclusive, to show that the declaration of Crawford was the original from which this portion of the letter was forged. These conclusions are considered at length in the next chapter. It must suffice here to state that the criticism of Hosack introduced such a strong element of doubt as, in the opinion of nearly all subsequent writers, to render impossible the acceptance of Letter 2 as genuine, although the doubt was not sufficient to warrant the absolute conclusion that the letter was a forgery. The influence of Hosack's criticism was augmented by his able summary of the difficulties that stood in the way of reconciling certain statements in this letter and in Letter 1 with the supposed shortness of Mary's stay in Glasgow. These difficulties, if not insuperable, are at least of such a kind as to demand serious and careful consideration.

Scarcely had the volume of Hosack been given to the world, when the existence of two more copies of the original French letters, Nos. 4 and 6, was made known by Baron Kervyn de Lettenhove, who, discovering them during a visit to Hatfield, published them in 1872 in the *Bulletin de l'Académie Royale de Belgique*, with a commentary entitled "Marie Stuart, d'après les documents conservés au Château de Hatfield." Baron de Lettenhove ingenuously states that his special reason for making the pilgrimage to Hatfield was the hope that he might discover some evidence to establish the innocence of the maligned Queen of Scots. He published the letters in the belief that they were forgeries, and that the world would share his opinion. It is quite plain, however, that his knowledge of the controversy was of a very superficial kind; and in such circumstances it was almost inevitable that his admittedly strong bias should lead him astray. A peculiarity of the copy of Letter 6 is that, unlike any of the other copies either at Hatfield or the Record Office, it is written in an Italian hand, not altogether dissimilar to that of Mary in her earlier years, but with corrections in another hand. Baron de Lettenhove, supposing that he had discovered one of the original Casket Letters, had it photographed along with another genuine letter of Mary's, in order that the difference of the penmanship between them—certainly very apparent

—might be detected. The editors of the Hatfield Calendar (vol. i., 1883) are very properly of opinion that it is only a copy, and probably only a copy of a copy. The fact that it has been merely endorsed by Cecil " frēch " (French) is almost in itself decisive, for with his careful accuracy it is impossible to conceive that he would not have described it as one of the original documents if it had really been one. In addition to this, there is also undoubted proof that none of the original documents in the casket were left with Cecil. Baron de Lettenhove also made some criticisms on peculiarities of style in both letters, with the view of showing that such letters could not have been written by Mary.

For ten years the real significance of the discovery of these additional French versions remained unrecognised, but the publication of the able paper by Dr. Harry Bresslau, "Die Kassettenbriefe der Königin Maria Stuart," in the *Historisches Taschenbuche* for 1882 again altered the whole situation. From this time the discussion of the Casket Letters question has, on the Continent — especially by German, but also by French writers — assumed a shape which renders many of Mr. Skelton's arguments entirely irrelevant. Writing in 1888, Mr. Skelton has deemed it sufficient to repeat substantially, and almost verbally, the same arguments against the letters that he made use of eighteen years ago. Some slight alterations which he has introduced, without any explanation, in order to harmonize his statements with altered views in regard to the character and policy of Maitland, will be referred to in a subsequent chapter. The following paragraph, however, comprehends all that he has deemed it necessary to state regarding the bearing of the discovery of contemporary copies on the genuineness of the letters: "Contemporary copies of certain of the letters have been preserved in two of our great libraries. Three are in the Record Office; three are at Hatfield. Of the letters in the Record Office which are supposed to incriminate the Queen, Mr. Markham Thorpe, who prepared the *Calendar of State Papers* relating to Scotland during her reign, emphatically declared, in his admirable introduction, that looked at in every light, they were open to the gravest suspicion —'abundance of insinuation, much assertion of guilt, but proof nowhere.' The members of the Historical Commission, who are preparing the Calendar of the Papers at Hatfield, have arrived substantially at the same conclusion; none of the series can be used, they say, as direct evidence against Mary, and some of them have been suspiciously manipulated. In these circumstances, an accomplished and impartial scholar like Mr. Mandell Creighton is driven to conclude that 'at present the balance of evidence seems to tend to the conclusion that the letters were forgeries.'"[1] The quotation from Professor Creighton's *Age of Elizabeth*—one

[1] *Maitland of Lethington*, ii. 334.

of the "Epochs of Modern History" series—is rather misleading, for the "at present" cannot properly be understood as referring to any other date than the year in which it was first issued, which was in 1874, or nine years before vol. i. of the Hatfield Papers was published. Nor does it contain any reference to the "circumstances" mentioned by Mr. Skelton. In regard to Markham Thorpe and the Historical Commissioners, Mr. Skelton has not succeeded in stating their views with sufficient accuracy. Thorpe's opinions are, of course, now rather out of date, for his preface to vol. i. of the *Calendar of Scottish State Papers* was written in 1858, just thirty years previous to the publication of Mr. Skelton's volume; but, in addition to this, the remarks of Thorpe quoted by Mr. Skelton do not refer specially to the Casket Letters, but to the whole series of papers on Mary Queen of Scots, including those connected with the Babington conspiracy. Whether Thorpe's remarks are just is another matter; but, so far as the Casket Letters are concerned, they are sufficiently explained when he states specifically in regard to them,—first, "that they are not in Queen Mary's handwriting" (as of course they are not); and secondly, "that there is not, in the State Papers here described, any one which shows participation on the Queen's part in the murder of Darnley."[1]

The references of the Historical Commissioners to

[1] Preface, *Calendar Scottish State Papers*, vol. i. p. 26.

the various versions of the letters indicate that they have to some extent misunderstood the main question at issue. They, nevertheless, express themselves with considerable caution, and their words cannot be made to bear the interpretation put upon them by Mr. Skelton. They, indeed, affirm that the letter in Italian hand, *if original*, has been "suspiciously manipulated," an undeniable proposition, for corrections have been made on it in another hand; and that "none of the series can be adduced as direct evidence against Mary," but the sole reason they give for the latter opinion is, "that not one is an original document, all being copies, and probably copies of copies." Neither the Historical Commissioners nor Mr. Skelton have apparently recognised that the existence of these copies of the original French letters, and of English copies of others, has entirely demolished Goodall's theory, and all the inferences dependent upon it. It has established beyond the smallest question, that the French version of the letters published by Cumez in 1573 was not the French version produced at Westminster. Thus, Goodall's demonstration that the published French version was a translation, so far from proving that Mary did not write the letters produced at Westminster, only enables us to distinguish more clearly between the two French versions—the original and the translated one. In view of the existence of these copies of the original French letters entirely differing from those which Mr.

Skelton asserts were supplied by Cecil to the French translator, the assumption—still persisted in by Mr. Skelton—that Cecil or Buchanan supplied the original copies "which were in their own hands" to the French translator; that these published French versions were "exact reproductions, made at the time, of the letters produced at Westminster;" and that in these published versions "we have in every case the letters produced at Westminster,"[1] must at least awaken astonishment at the strength and staunchness of his convictions. The publication of Dr. Bresslau's paper excited very wide interest on the Continent, especially in Germany, where it has originated a new Casket controversy, in connection with which a great variety of ingenious theories have been promulgated. Among these may be mentioned the theory of Gerdes,[2] that Letter 1 was written by Darnley to Mary, and that part of Letter 2 was written by Mary to her brother Moray; and the theory of Dr. Bernard Sepp, that the main portions of the letters were taken from a diary written by the Scottish Queen.[3] In view of the evidence yet to be adduced in regard to the letters, the consideration of these theories need not now detain us. They are only referred to because they are the

[1] Vol. ii. 331.
[2] *Geschichte der Königin Maria Stuart*, 1885.
[3] *Tagebuch der unglücklichen Schotten Königin Maria Stuart*, 1882.

theories of strenuous supporters of Mary, and because they show that by general consent the theory of Goodall is now ignored in Germany as entirely exploded.

The copies of the original French versions[1] of the letters now known to exist are Nos. 3 and 5 in the Record Office, and Nos. 4 and 6 at Hatfield. Of these only No. 6 can be regarded as in itself fatally compromising. At the Record Office there are English translations of Nos. 1, 2, and 5, and at Hatfield English translations of Nos. 4 and 6; Nos. 7 and 8 only exist in the printed versions. The alterations and corrections on these copies of the letters have aroused some conscientious distrust on the part of the compilers of the Calendars of State Papers and others, who have gravely expressed the opinion that therefore the copies cannot be regarded as correct transcripts, or, in the case of the translations, sufficiently trustworthy renderings, of the original letters. Yet, so far from there being anything suspicious in the character of the alterations, they must actually be regarded as the best possible guarantee of correctness. They are written generally in another hand than that of the copyist, and, in not a few instances, in the hand of Cecil. In the case of the French copies, they merely correct a mistaken reading of the original manuscript, and, in the case of the translations, supply a better rendering of the meaning. That this is the explanation of the

[1] See Appendix C, p. 121.

alterations might have been conjectured, but we are not left to mere conjecture, for in the minutes of the Commission it is distinctly stated that, after the copies had been made, they "were read in French, and a due collation made thereof, as neere as could be by reading and inspection, and made to accord with the originals, which the said Earl of Murray required to be redelivered, and did thereupon deliver the copies being collationed."[1] In view of this very clear and definite declaration, the copies of the letters in the State Paper Office and at Hatfield must be regarded as thoroughly authenticated transcripts of the original documents contained in the casket.

After an exhaustive comparison of the phrases and turns of style of the four French letters with those of genuine letters of Mary in Labanoff's collection, Dr. Bresslau not only found in the accepted letters of Mary parallel peculiarities to most of those adduced by Baron de Lettenhove as casting suspicion on the genuineness of the Casket Letters, but also arrived at the conclusion, from the special and peculiar idioms of the four letters, that they must have been written by Mary. In regard to the famous Letter 2, — the original French version of which has not yet been discovered, — Dr. Bresslau has concluded, from a comparison of the Scots and English versions, and a careful consideration of the idioms of each, that the greater

[1] Goodall, ii. 235.

part was originally written in French, probably by Mary; but he also holds that the portion corresponding to the declaration of Crawford is based on that declaration. Consequently he rejects Letter 2 as a forgery, based partly on an unknown composition of Mary, and partly on the declaration of Crawford. The evidence which leads him to reject the letter is entirely external, and practically identical with that which influenced Hosack. It will be considered in the next chapter. Meanwhile it may be remarked that Dr. Bresslau cannot be regarded as having established beyond question the genuineness of the four letters of Mary, for it has been shown that similar peculiarities of style to those adduced by him may be found in the letters of Catherine de Medici. The epistolary manner of Mary was that in vogue at this period among the ladies of the French Court. In addition to this, there is the likelihood that the forger—if they were forged — would carefully endeavour to imitate her peculiarities. Again, it has been argued that, if Letter 2 be rejected as a forgery, grave suspicion, to say the least, must attach to the others. This is undoubtedly true, but it is also clear that, if the genuineness of the four French letters be established, both is Mary fatally incriminated, and a presumption is created in favour of the genuineness of the others. The internal evidence adduced by Dr. Bresslau does not, however, seem to warrant conclusions of a more decisive kind than the following:—(1) That the French version of the letters, published in 1573, was in the case of none of the letters identical with the French version exhibited at Westminster; (2) that the Scots version of the letters was not the original one, but translated from the French; and (3) that the writer of the French version must have been thoroughly conversant with Mary's epistolary style—so conversant that there is no sufficient evidence in the style to disprove the theory that Mary was the author of them. These conclusions, so far as they have reference to Letter 2, are illustrated in the next chapter, where the external evidence bearing on its genuineness is also considered.

CHAPTER VI.

LETTER 2.

THE form and structure of Letter 2 are very peculiar, so peculiar as almost to necessitate the conclusion either that it was written by Mary, or founded on some original composition of hers. It is difficult to understand a forger constructing such a letter without the suggestion of some original document, and it is also difficult to understand why he should have retained so much of the original form of the composition, for by doing so he was leaving a very palpable clue—a clue so palpable as almost to render detection inevitable. On the other hand, few persons will be disposed to cavil at the opinion expressed by Mr. Skelton, "that such another love-letter does not exist." In the middle of the letter there is something resembling a table of contents,—a most extraordinary interpolation in a letter,—but this is explained towards the close by the words: "I had na paper when I wrat that of ye memoriall." The meaning these words seem intended to convey is, that Mary had jotted down certain things about which she intended to inform

Bothwell, but, not being able at the time to procure more paper, had begun the letter itself on the same sheet. Supposing the letter to have been a forgery, it must have been carefully shaped and fashioned so as to correspond with this statement. At the end of the letters there is what Mr. Skelton defines as "another table of contents, which contains, *inter alia*, this unaccountable intimation: 'Remember me of the Lord Bothwell'!" It apparently did not occur to Mr. Skelton that forgers would be unlikely to insert such an "unaccountable intimation" as he describes. The intimation, or whatever it may be called, is not "Remember *me* of the Lord Bothwell," but "Remember *zou*," etc., and it does not form part of a table of contents, but of directions, presumedly on the back of the letter, to aid the memory of the messenger.

In regard to the style and structure of the letter, the opinions of those who accept it as genuine differ of course very widely from the opinions of those who regard it as a forgery. Perhaps the most extreme opinion on the one side is that of Mr. Froude, that it "could have been invented only by a genius equal to that of Shakespeare;"[1] and, on the other, that of Mr. Skelton, that "a rustic wench trying painfully to write a letter to a sweetheart would have succeeded better," and that it is "a singular and incoherent jumble."[2] If Mr. Froude has expressed

---

[1] *History of England*, Cabinet edition, vii. 502.
[2] *Maitland of Lethington*, ii. 336.

himself too unguardedly in one direction, Mr. Skelton's description perhaps surpasses even the limits of legitimate burlesque. Hosack in his criticism was more restrained than Mr. Skelton. All that he ventured to affirm was, that there was a striking difference in tone between the earlier and latter half of the letter, the one being fierce and reckless, and the other full of remorse; and that both pictures appeared to be overdrawn, the one being that of a person almost devoid of common feeling, and the other that of a person whose conscience was remarkably sensitive and tender. This criticism is measured, reasonable, and worthy of consideration, but it can scarcely be regarded as fatally damaging. The very variety of moods portrayed in the letter is an evidence rather of its genuineness than of the reverse; and since such acute and able critics as Hume, Robertson, Mignet, Froude, and Charles Kingsley have not discerned in the literary structure and general tone of the letter anything inconsistent with its genuineness, we are driven to conclude, on the supposition that it was a forgery, either that it was in great part identical with an original composition of Mary's, or that the forger was a person both of very exceptional literary skill and very remarkable knowledge of human character and motives. In regard to what has been styled an occasional "coarseness of tone" in the letter, it must be taken into consideration that the Scottish language is a much less delicate instrument of expression than French, and that the Scots translator probably exaggerated any suggestions of coarseness in the original. In some instances he also misread the original words: the phrase "the devil sinder us"—which led a defender of Mary to point out that Mary would never refer to the Catholic Church under such a simile—is rendered in English "the good year sever us." Possibly the French was "le bon Dieu." On another passage Mr. Skelton comments thus: "Then there are passages so offensively unsavoury (as that which describes how Lord Livingstone took her about the body when she was warming herself against him) that they could only have been written by a woman who had forfeited her self-respect, and lost all sense of decency." What the other passages are is nowhere stated by Mr. Skelton; but in the case of this particular one, which he also terms "eminently nasty," the unsavouriness has unwittingly been added chiefly by himself. The words in the English version are, "when I was leaning upon him and warming myself;" and in the Scots version, "when I was lenand upon him warming me at the fire." In neither version do the words "against him" occur. They have been supplied by Mr. Skelton; and the words "at the fyre" in the Scotch version, which he has accepted as the original, shows that he is entirely mistaken in the interpretation he has put upon the language.

One remarkable characteristic of the letter is the

minuteness of its references to Mary's private affairs, and to other circumstances which could not have been known to any but those in her company at Glasgow. The theory that this information was communicated to Captain Thomas Crawford through Darnley, is an inadequate explanation of the presence of these details. The following are the principal matters about which a forger would require to obtain special information :—The meeting with Crawford four miles from Glasgow; her conversation with him; her meeting with Sir James Hamilton, and Hamilton's conversation; the arrival of the Laird of Luss and others; her statement regarding her isolation in Glasgow; the references of Darnley to her "stait," to her taking Paris (Hubert) and Gilbert, to the sending away of Joseph (see letter of Joseph Riccio to Joseph Lutyni in *Cal. State Papers*, Scot. ser., i. 242), and to the marriage of Bastian; other conversations with Darnley in regard even to matters not mentioned by Crawford in his declaration; and the conversation with Lord Livingstone after supper. Not all the matters above mentioned could have been communicated to the forgers by Crawford; and it was very hazardous to detail such conversations as those with Sir James Hamilton and Lord Livingstone if they never took place, for both Sir James Hamilton and Lord Livingstone would have detected the forgery as soon as the letter was produced. To support the thesis that the letter is a forgery, the original document theory is thus rendered as essential as the theory that a portion of the letter was founded on Crawford's declaration.

Dr. Bresslau was driven to adopt the original document theory from evidences both in the Scots and English versions, indicating that the greater part of the letter was a translation from a French original. A minute examination of the letter seems, however, also to show that it must throughout—even in the portion Dr. Bresslau supposes to have been founded on Crawford's declaration—have originally been written in French; and, moreover, the texture and structure of the whole document, the sentiments, purposes, and proposals expressed in it, especially in the latter half, render it almost inevitably compromising, even on the supposition that it is only in a very fractional sense the composition of Mary. The influence of a French original throughout the whole letter is shown by either the presence of French idioms, mistranslation of French words or phrases, direct appropriation of French words, or selection of English or Scotch words nearly similar to French words, and used in a sense which seems to have been more or less suggested by the French signification. The following examples in that small portion of the letter which most nearly corresponds with the declaration of Crawford come under one or other of these headings. In the English version, "you have them well pardoned," the "well" being neither in the Scots nor the published French version; in the English version "and mysse of promis," and in the Scots version "inlacke of his promeis," probably, both in the Scots and English versions, influenced by the French "promesse;" in the Scots version, "I shall never make fault," and in English, "I will not make fault"—French "faire faute;" in the English version, the idiom "I am punished to have made my God of you;" in the Scots version, "I might playne unto zow," probably suggested by the French; both in the Scots and English versions, "not being familiar with you"—French "familier;" in the Scots version, "necessity constrains me;" in the Scots version, "I answerit ay unto him"—French, "Je lui répondis toujours." It ought to be kept in mind that none of the phrases above mentioned occur in Crawford's declaration. Leaving this especially disputed portion of the letter, we find in another portion of the English version at the Record Office two remarkable proofs that the original document contained some very idiomatic French. In explanation of a mistranslation in the English version, "I may do much without you,"—which had apparently puzzled the Scotch translator, for it is omitted in the Scotch version,—Cecil has written on the margin the original French, "J'ay bien la vogue avec vous;" and in the English version also occur the words, "I have taken the worms out of his nose," a literal translation of a French phrase, "tirer les vers du nez," which in the Scotch version is rendered, "I have drawn it all out of him." The beginning of the letter, "Estant party du lieu ou j'avois laissé mon cœur il se peult aysement juger quelle estoit ma contenance," etc., which is of course in the original French, has also been shown by Dr. Bresslau to correspond very closely in phrase and structure with the beginning of a genuine letter of Mary's in Labanoff's collection. Dr. Bernard Sepp also, who writes in defence of Mary, has, on account of idioms and phrases in the English and Scots versions of the letter, which he supposes derived from French idioms and phrases closely corresponding with those in genuine letters of Mary, come to the conclusion that the document was in great part a composition of Mary. His ingenious theory scarcely demands consideration here, even if it did not rest on possibly deceptive evidence. For the present argument it is only necessary to show that the English and Scots versions throughout are taken from a French original, and that this original, for all that appears to the contrary in the structure of these versions, might have been written by Mary.

The following illustrations of the influence of a French original are given in the order in which they occur in the letter—the portion of the letter corresponding to the declaration of Crawford being omitted as having been already examined:—In the English version, "durst not enterprise so to do," and in the Scotch, "enterpryse the same," the word enterprise being probably suggested by the French; in the Scots version "summa," which occurs several times, from the French " en somme," a common phrase of Mary's; English, " for the rest it were too long," etc.; Scots, " would have persewit him," translated in English " would have followed;" English, "accompany himself with the Hamiltons," in Scots, " accompanyit him," etc.; English, the French spelling "Stuart"; Scots, " gif I had maid my estait," French, " état," inventory; English, " the place shall continue till death," and in the Scots, " the place shall hold unto the death " (Hosack comments: " Place in the Scotch means castle or place of strength. It is correctly translated in the French version of the letter 'fortresse.'" Apparently he was ignorant that the French word "place" meant fortress. Instances of the appropriation of the word in this sense occasionally occur in Scots of the fifteenth century, but this usage did not become acclimatized); Scots version, " that false race that will travell no less with zow for the same," this use of the word " travell," translated in the English " work," being probably suggested by the French " travailler;" the phrase, " I believe they have been at school together," a too literal rendering of the French, " faire une école;" Scots, " makis pieteous caressing," where " fawning " would have been a more correct, but not so literal translation; Scots, " ges quhat presage that is," rendered in English " guess what token that is;" Scots, " This is my first jornay," and English, " This is my first journay," both being a mistranslation of the French "journée," which undoubtedly means in this case "day" or "day's work;" Scots, "I sall end my bybill," English, "will end my bible," apparently in both cases a misreading of the French "billet;" English, "I am weary and am asleep," the "am asleep" being a mistranslation for "am sleepy;" Scots, "of my estait," English, "of my state;" Scots, "of Monsiure de Levingstoun;" Scots, "quhilk is couplit underneath with twa courdonis," rendered in English, "which is tyed with two laces;" Scots, "because for haist it was made," the "for" indicating the influence of the French "pour;" Scots, "But I remit me altogidder to zour will," and in English, "I remitt myself wholly to your will;" Scots, "Send me advertisement quhat I sall do," rendered in English, "Send me word what I shall do;" Scots, "Advise to with yourself," apparently from French, "avisez-vous," translated in English "think;" Scots, the phrase "summa, for certainty he suspects of the thing ye knaw and of hys lyif." English, "For that that I can learn;" Scots, "As towart the Lady Reres," rendered in English, "And even touching the Lady Reres;" Scots, "I pray God that scho may serve zow for your honour," and in English, "God grant that she serve to your honour," both phrases indicating the influence of a French idiom; Scots, "becaus of the refuse I maid of his offers." Scots, "It is ready to thame," rendered in English, "It is ready thereunto;" Scots, "I fear it will bring some malheur;" Scots, "He inrages when he hears

F

of Lethington;" Scots, "Of your brother he speaks nathyng," the inversion being peculiarly French; Scots, "I wyll make you memorial at evin;" Scots, "Nathing but fascherie," translated in English, "Nothing but upon grief;" Scots, "Se not hir," and in English, "See not also her," apparently a somewhat awkward translation of the French "regarder;" Scots, "I sustene for to merite hir place;" Scots, "obtaining the which against my naturel," rendered in English, "my own nature;" and Scots, "that may impesche me."

These few examples, which appear on the very surface of the letter, are sufficient to show that, even in its most compromising portions, it was originally written in French; and thus they very powerfully supplement the weight of the other internal evidence for its genuineness. The external evidence against its genuineness is comprehended entirely under two heads: the close correspondence of the declaration of Captain Thomas Crawford, Darnley's servant, with a portion of the letter, and the improbability that Mary could, during the period of her stay in Glasgow, have written and despatched both this letter and Letter 1 in the manner alluded to in the letters.

In regard to the objection arising from the close correspondence of the portion of the letter with a portion of Crawford's declaration, it is to be observed that, while the indications in the letter of a translation from a French original would seem to indicate that it is not borrowed from the declaration, the absence of the influence of a French original in this portion of the declaration favours the theory that Crawford did not borrow it from the letter, but wrote it down from his recollections of Darnley's communication. The striking and special dissimilarity now mentioned is, in fact, entirely opposed to the theory of collusion. But does this dissimilarity completely counterbalance the argument that may be drawn from the close correspondence in other respects of these portions of the two documents? As Mr. Skelton has ventured "to affirm that the two most skilful reporters in the world, sitting side by side, and recording the words as they fell from the lips of the speakers, could not have preserved a more perfect verbal accord,"[1] it is necessary to point out that, though the two records correspond very closely, not only in regard to subject matter, but to sequence of thought, the correspondence is very far indeed from being verbal. Moreover, the closely corresponding portions relate almost wholly to a single consecutive statement of Darnley made to Mary on her returning to him after dinner. It is explanatory of his position and attitude towards her, and bears evidence of having been carefully prepared beforehand. Indeed, it is by no means an improbable supposition that its general tenor had even been suggested by Crawford, with whom he was on specially confidential terms. Mary's accurate recollection of the statement would scarcely

[1] ii. 341.

have been wonderful even in ordinary circumstances; but, with her mental energies in a state of peculiar tension, it is only natural to suppose that all the details of the interview were photographed on her mental retina with peculiar distinctness. To illustrate the impossibility of such a degree of similarity between the two records without collusion, Hosack gives a quotation from two very dissimilar summarized reports—the one that of the *Times* and the other that of the *Telegraph*—of the speech of the Lord Chief Justice in the case Saurin *v.* Star, on 27th Feb. 1869. Apart, however, from the objection that the reports are condensed summaries, and that the legal reporter of the *Times* was no doubt a barrister, while the *Telegraph* reporter probably knew nothing of law, the illustration proves nothing more than that two persons may report the same thing very differently. This proposition is sufficiently credible without the aid of any illustration, but it does not in the least tend to show that no two persons will, under any condition, give a very similar account of the same statement. Nor, on the supposition that there was collusion, is it proved that the record of Crawford was the original one. Crawford, indeed, affirmed, and not improbably with truth, that for the information of Lennox he wrote down at the time what Darnley reported as having passed between him and the Queen; but these documents had apparently been destroyed, and it is by no means improbable that Crawford refreshed his recollection by the aid of the letter, which, in any case, he may have seen before he prepared his statement. Probably he would have been ready to have admitted this. Hosack and those who support his theory suppose the forgery to have taken place subsequent to the flight of Queen Mary into England, and point to the fact that Lennox on the 11th June 1568 wrote to Crawford to use every means to obtain further evidence against the Queen of Scots, and especially to obtain correct information as to the date of her visit to Glasgow to fetch Darnley. They suppose that the information supplied by Crawford in answer to that letter furnished important materials for the concoction of Letter 2. Morton's declaration, to be considered in the next chapter, has an important bearing on the truth of this hypothesis. Meantime, it is sufficient to state that the letters produced in the Parliament of December 1567 were of such a kind as sufficiently to incriminate the Queen; that there is no proof of their having undergone the supposed alteration; and that the Scots version of the letters was placed in the hands of Mr. John Wood when he was about to set out to England, on the 22nd June 1568, or within ten days of the letter of Lennox to Crawford.

Letter 2, if genuine, must, from internal evidence, have been written from Glasgow; and the letter known as No. 1 is dated from Glasgow, Saturday, in the morning. The references in Letter 2 show that it ought more properly to be designated

Letter 1, for it must have been begun, if not finished and despatched, before the letter written on Saturday morning. Saturday was the 25th of January, and a cardinal point is whether Mary arrived soon enough in Glasgow to permit of the composition of the long letter known as No. 2. If reliance is to be placed on dates in the Privy Seal Register, this was impossible, for it shows that Mary signed deeds, dated at Edinburgh, on the 22nd and 24th of January. Apart from other evidence contradicting these dates, their conclusiveness is impaired by the fact that it is the testimony of the accused person; that she subsequently dated similar documents at Edinburgh while she was at Dunbar; and that as, according to the evidence of the same Register, she had arrived at Linlithgow on her return by the 28th, her stay in Glasgow would have been too short to have permitted her accomplishing her purpose of arranging that Darnley should return with her. Moreover, these dates are contradicted by the separate diaries of two Edinburgh citizens, Robert Birrel, and the author of the *Diurnal of Remarkable Occurrents*, both of whom give the 20th January as the date of her departure from Edinburgh. The fact that in the Register of the Great Seal a large number of grants are dated on the 20th, and that no subsequent entries occur there until after her return from Glasgow, seems also to indicate that she left Edinburgh either on the 20th or 21st. The latter is the date mentioned in the prepared journal or diary handed in by the Scottish Commissioners to Cecil. From the fact that Lennox wrote the letter referred to on p. 85, it is evident that the date at least of Mary's arrival in Glasgow was founded on information supplied by Thomas Crawford; but, as the means of fixing dates after an interval of a year and a half were by no means so plentiful in those days, when no newspaper existed, and perpetual references to precise dates were not so necessary as now, Crawford's inquiries would be prosecuted under such difficulties as to render absolute correctness scarcely possible. The preference ought, therefore, decidedly to be given to the date of the Edinburgh diarists, who made their entries when the events they recorded took place. Apparently convinced that the testimony of the Register of the Privy Seal was inadmissible, or that, if admissible, it proved too much, Hosack took his stand on what he termed Mary's accusers' own ground—that she set out from Edinburgh on the 21st and arrived in Glasgow on the 23rd. The long Glasgow letter, Hosack asserted, could not have been begun on the night of Mary's arrival, because of the reference to Darnley confessing about Hiegate on "the morne after" her arrival; and because of the words, "the king sent for Joachim yesternight." He therefore infers that the letter could not have been begun before the evening of the 24th; and as there is internal evidence that it could not have been finished before late on the following evening, it is necessary to make the absurd supposition that, while the composition of the long letter was in progress, she wrote and despatched the short letter on the Saturday morning. The expressions on which Hosack's argument is based occur only in the Scots translation, and, although the reference to Hiegate in the Scots translation is more comprehensible than the reference in the English translation, there is no proof that it is more correct, for the Hiegate episode is a somewhat obscure one, the only other reference to it being in a letter of Mary to the Archbishop of Glasgow. Moreover, there are other references in the letter to indicate that it was commenced on the night of Mary's arrival, such as, "This is my first jornay" (day's work), "I went my way to sup," "I will speak to him to-morrow on that point," following a record of the first interview. But, in addition to this, the dates in the diaries of the two Edinburgh citizens render it not impossible that Mary arrived in Glasgow as early even as the 21st; and in any case, all things considered, the 22nd is a more probable date than the 23rd. Certain statements of French Paris (Hubert) would indicate that the letter was despatched on the 24th, but it has been objected that his confession was obtained in a suspicious manner, and is insufficiently attested. In any case, his statements cannot be accepted as unimpeachable, and therefore may be left out of consideration, especially as his confession was made subsequent to the Westminster Conference.

The result obtained by the examination of the external as well as the internal evidence in regard to Letter 2, if chiefly negative, is thus not at all negative in the sense of disproving its genuineness. The value of the conclusion arrived at will become apparent after a consideration of Morton's declaration.

CHAPTER VII.

MORTON'S DECLARATION.

MORTON's Declaration, like the Casket Documents, has been lost, and until the publication of the Fifth Report of the Historical Manuscripts Commission no copy of it was known to exist. The Commissioners gave what appeared to be a succinct summary of the document, but it is a summary resembling a description of the play of Hamlet without any reference to Hamlet himself. In 1883 the manuscripts of Sir Alexander Malet were acquired by the Trustees of the British Museum, and the copy of the Declaration of Morton — which had been summarized by the Historical Commissioners — now forms folio 216 of No. 32,091 of the Additional MSS. Being desirous to know whether Morton merely declared in vague and general terms that he had opened the casket in presence of "others," as the Historical MSS. Commission's Report has it, or whether the names of those present were given, I carefully examined the manuscript, and found it to contain statements of such vital consequence as practically to be decisive in regard to the authenticity of the documents. The

Declaration is printed in full in Appendix A. Its graphic and detailed picture of what, if it really happened, was a very striking historical incident, bears, at least, all the external marks of truth. The copy is a contemporary one, and of its genuineness there can be no doubt whatever. The two cardinal points in the declaration are, (1) that the documents, immediately after the casket was opened, were "sichted," and (2) the list of the noblemen and others by whom, Morton affirmed, they were "sichted."

The Scots verb to "sicht" is somewhat analogous to the German "sichten," and is defined by Jamieson as "to view narrowly, to inspect." Jamieson illustrates its meaning by the two following examples: "The Moderator craved that these books might be sighted by Argyle, Lauderdale, and Southesk" (Baillie's *Letters*, i. 113); "At this assembly Dr. Sibbald late minister of Aberdeen his papers which were taken from him were revised and sighted; some whereof smacked of Arminianism as they thought, and whilk they kept" (Spalding, i. 135). The word was a technical, almost a legal term, applied specially to the inspection of documents. If the documents in the casket underwent such a process of inspection on the 21st June 1567, it was practically impossible that they could have been afterwards exchanged for forged documents without the fraud being detected. In such an extraordinary crisis of affairs it was of the utmost importance for the Confederate Lords to know the precise tenor of the documents thus stated to have been discovered. Supposing the examination to have been *bona fide*, the casket would be opened with the utmost curiosity, and the documents read and considered with the greatest care. Even if there be the possibility that some of the documents were afterwards manipulated and altered, it is impossible to suppose that such an extraordinary document as Letter 2, containing the main portion of the incriminating evidence against the Queen, could have been fabricated subsequently, or that the two contracts of marriage could have been subsequently placed in the casket.

What proof, then, did Morton adduce that they were "sichted"? A list of witnesses very formidable in numbers, and in regard to individuals as formidable almost as it could possibly have been. The names, in addition to that of Morton, are :—the Earls of Atholl, Mar, and Glencairn, Lords Home, Semple, and Sanquhar, the Master of Graham, the Secretary (Maitland of Lethington), the Laird of Tullibardine, and Mr. Andrew Douglas. One peculiarity about the names, worthy of special notice, is that not one of them, with the exception of Morton, is affixed to the bond—as printed in Calderwood's *History of the Church of Scotland*—in favour of Bothwell signed in Ainslie's Tavern. It would have been egregious folly in Morton to have inserted in the list of those present at the "sichting" of the documents the names of any who were not present, or who were not prepared to assert that they were present. Such a fraud would inevitably, sooner or later, have been detected. In any case, the Regent and Morton, however daring they might be, were too sagacious to run such a tremendous risk. They were by no means certain of their position with Elizabeth—indeed, certainty on such a point was an absolute impossibility. On the supposition that Mary did not write the letters, they were, by giving in a false list of witnesses, supplying the most certain means of detection. Moreover, among the English noblemen before whom the whole of the papers were laid were those who, in the words of Mr. Froude, " had made themselves most conspicuous as the advocates of the Queen of Scots," including the Catholic Earls of Norfolk, Westmoreland, and Northumberland. But before these Catholic nobles of England Morton ventured to adduce Atholl, the leader of the Catholics of Scotland, and several other Catholic noblemen, as witnesses for the genuineness of the documents. Nor did he know, when he gave in his declaration on the 9th December, what exact turn the discussion might take; the English Commissioners, or any one of them, might have declined to accept the declaration unless confirmed by special inquiry of the persons mentioned; it was even then by no means impossible that Mary—especially if she did not write the letters—would agree to some form of inquiry which would lead to the whole evidence being placed before her. On any supposition, therefore, it is impossible to believe that Morton adduced as witnesses persons who were not present or were not prepared to swear that they were present.

But Atholl's testimony is almost of itself conclusive of the inspection of the documents. He had left the party of the Queen from entirely disinterested motives, and, being a Catholic, it is impossible to conceive that he would knowingly conspire to blast the reputation of a Catholic sovereign. Besides, he again became the leader of the Catholics in their policy against the Regency, and ultimately was one of Morton's most bitter enemies; but there is no evidence that he ever on any occasion expressed doubts regarding the genuineness of the Casket Documents, although the exposure of the forgery would have rendered an almost inestimable service to the cause of the Queen. Among other witnesses who subsequently supported the Queen were Lord Home, who joined Kirkaldy of Grange in the romantic defence of the Castle of Edinburgh, and who is described by Sir James Melville as "so true a Scotsman that he was unwinnable to England to do anything prejudicial to his country." The Deposition of Lord Home[1] in regard to the Regent Moray is entirely consistent with Sir James Melville's estimate, and both it and the Deposition of Kirkaldy of Grange must be held to refute the surmise of Mr. Skelton, that Kirkaldy of Grange, Lord Home, or any other leading supporter of Moray, left Moray because in producing the Casket Letters he had "lent

[1] See Appendix B, p. 117.

himself to a fraud." The other names include two Catholics,—Semple and the Laird of Tullibardine; Sanquhar, who, with Tullibardine, signed the bond for Mary's deliverance from Lochleven; and the Master of Graham, who, as the third Earl of Montrose, conspired with Argyll and Atholl to bring about Morton's fall in 1578, and afterwards had a prominent share in bringing him to the scaffold. In addition to these names, special importance attaches to the name of the Earl of Mar, whom Sir James Melville specially characterizes as a "trew nobleman," and who, by his moderation and fairness of spirit, had won the high respect of both parties. The testimony of these noblemen must be accepted as decisive at least regarding the fact of the "sichting" of the documents. If the documents were forged, the forgery must have been completed before that date. Lord Herries, the advocate of Queen Mary, while admitting the discovery of the casket, asserted that Morton had exchanged genuine documents for false ones. If he did so, this must have happened on the night of the 20th. There is, of course, the initial difficulty that Morton did not have the key, which was presumedly in the possession of Bothwell; but, in any case, the exchange could not have been effected in the presence of the noblemen above mentioned.

The character and position of perhaps the most notable witness to the "sichting" of the documents, namely, Maitland of Lethington, remain yet to be considered. Maitland was present both at the York and Westminster Conferences, but even by his colleagues he was distrusted: "all Scotland knew," in the words of Mr. Skelton, "that Maitland was on Mary's side;" he had been nicknamed by the Regent and his friends "the necessary evil;" the Regent, it was well known, had brought him with him to England, because he did not deem it safe to leave him at home; and, as a matter of fact, the Queen of Scots had, through his wife, Mary Fleming,—one of the "Queen's Maries,"—been secretly supplied with a copy of one of the versions of the letters. Notwithstanding Maitland's ambiguous attitude, Morton did not hesitate to declare on his solemn oath, in Maitland's presence, that the message regarding the mission of Bothwell's servants to the castle was sent to him while he was dining with Maitland in Edinburgh; that he gave orders for their apprehension in Maitland's presence; that the putting of George Dalgleish to the torture was resolved on "by common consent of the noblemen convened," including, of course, Maitland; and that Maitland was present when the casket was opened on the 21st. By this declaration, made in Maitland's presence, the word of Maitland was pledged, with an implication almost as absolute as that of Morton, for the genuineness of the documents. Referring to Maitland's attitude towards the accusations against Mary at the Conference, Mr. Skelton arrogates the right to assert that he "held

himself aloof from the farce that was being played."
Maitland's aloofness could not have been more than
moral or intellectual, for bodily he was present,
though possibly against his will. In view of
Morton's declaration, the hypothesis even of mental
or moral aloofness can scarcely, however, be
regarded any longer as specially appropriate.
Whether he wished it or not, the declaration of
Morton compelled Maitland to play a very prominent part in the farce, if it is to be reckoned a
farce. Maitland must also be held chiefly responsible
for the fact that the farce, if it was a farce, ended
in such a mournful tragedy. Some fatal spell
prevented him from uttering a syllable of protest
or explanation when Morton made the explicit
and detailed declaration virtually to the effect that
Maitland knew as much about the documents as
he did. It can hardly be maintained, on the
supposition that the letters were a forgery, that
this most skilled diplomatist, and, according to Mr.
Skelton, the ablest man, at that time, in Scotland,
if not even in Europe, was not completely
outwitted; or that he was not made to act a
part so sorry and contemptible as to cause Mr.
Skelton's eulogies on his character and abilities to
sound like subtle irony. Had he only on this all-
momentous occasion exhibited a faint gleam of that
"scorn of pharisaic pretence," which, according to
Mr. Skelton, "scorched like fire," how withering
would have been the effect on Morton and his

accomplices! The theory of Mr. Skelton seems to be that Maitland was "not a party to the deceit," and was ignorant of its innermost secret. On this theory Maitland might have allowed Morton to tell his own tale, provided he refrained from falsehoods as to Maitland's connection with the discovery of the casket; but to allow Morton to associate him so circumstantially with the opening of the casket was, if Morton forswore himself, to witness without an apparent symptom of regret the extinguishment of the last flicker of his own honour. Diplomacy, it is true, has its own peculiar canons, but no canon, however "exceeding broad," can either excuse or explain such callous torpidity. But even were we to regard as possible the theory that Maitland in such extraordinary circumstances "would not have acted otherwise than he did," it is impossible to suppose that the Regent and Morton had made such a theory the basis of their action, and that, if there was a damning secret, they were trusting to Maitland's eternal retention of it, except possibly on one of two suppositions — either that Maitland was concerned in the forgery, or was afraid of the consequences of his implication in Darnley's murder.

That Maitland was the forger has been a favourite theory with those who deny the genuineness of the documents. This theory was even at one time held by Mr. Skelton: "The master wit of Lethington," he said, "was there to shape the plot; Lethington, with numberless scraps of the Queen's handwriting in his possession, and with a divine or diabolic spark of genius in his nature, which might have made him on a large scale one of the leaders of mankind."[1] Although Mr. Skelton has not penned any recantation of this opinion republished in 1876, it must be presumed that later information has led him to regard it as no longer tenable; for in the second volume of *Maitland of Lethington*, published in 1888, the above theory is silently suppressed in favour of the Morton theory—"dissolute lawyers and unfrocked priests" being summoned by Mr. Skelton's imagination to execute the task for which the services of Maitland's "divine or diabolic" genius are no longer available. "Morton," he remarks, "one of the mercenaries of the Reformation, who, like others of his trade, combined craft with ferocity, had plenty of clever scamps in his pay—dissolute lawyers, unfrocked priests—who, out of the mass of Mary's manuscripts which were found at Holyrood, could have manufactured with facility a score of letters to a lover."[2] Whether the Morton theory, as stated by Mr. Skelton, with its whole bundle of assumptions, be regarded as more credible or not than the Maitland theory, the latter theory has not only been abandoned, but entirely refuted by Mr. Skelton. If in his volumes on Maitland of Lethington he has demonstrated

[1] *The Impeachment of Mary Stuart*, p. 209.
[2] *Maitland of Lethington*, ii. 305.

anything, he has demonstrated that Maitland was incapable of committing such a forgery, or being an active party to such a conspiracy against the Queen of Scots. One of the main purposes of his volumes is to illustrate the fact that Maitland had always the best interests of the Queen at heart; and it would be straining our credulity too far to ask us to believe that Maitland had recourse to the forgery of the Casket Documents to promote the Queen's best interests. Opinions may differ as to whether Mr. Skelton has not formed too high an opinion of Maitland both morally and intellectually, both as a churchman and as a statesman, but it can scarcely be doubted that he has been successful in removing from Maitland's reputation much undeserved obloquy, and in demonstrating that he was at least as consistent and unselfish in his conduct as the majority of politicians. Such a view of Maitland's character cannot be maintained if he had any connection with the forgery of the letters, and, even if it could, the fact that the forgery must have been completed before the 20th June renders it impossible that he could have had any part in it. He had left the Queen as late as the 9th, and Morton was too prudent to have accepted the services of such a recruit in such a compromising enterprise. Indeed, there can scarcely be any doubt that Maitland only stated the truth in regard to his attitude to Mary at this time, when in a letter to Cecil of the 21st June (written probably immediately after the discovery of the

Casket Documents), he said: "The reverence and affection I have ever borne to the Queen, my mistress, hath been the occasion to stay me so long in company with the Earl of Bothwell at the Court, —as my life hath every day been in danger since he began to aspire to any grandeur."

It being thus impossible to conceive that Maitland was directly concerned in the concoction of the forgery, it remains to be considered whether his silent assent to Morton's declaration is explicable on the supposition of his implication in the murder of Darnley. In regard to Maitland's connection with the murder, Mr. Skelton has arrived at a verdict of "not proven." This is certainly to take the most favourable view possible of Maitland's conduct, and, in arriving at it, Mr. Skelton has omitted any reference to the testimony of Bothwell's subordinate agents in regard to the Craigmillar bond. For verdicts of "not proven"—a peculiarity of Scots law—Mr. Skelton has a peculiar *penchant*, except where the opponents of Mary are concerned. In regard to the heinous guilt of Moray, Morton, Knox, Cecil, and Elizabeth, he is untroubled by the smallest scruples of doubt; but the evidence must be very unimpeachable indeed that will compel him to admit any definite wrong-doing either in the case of Mary or of Maitland. That Maitland was directly involved in the plot against Darnley is at least more probable than that Moray or any of his more intimate colleagues was involved in it. He differed from them, however, in that he never disguised his dislike to Mary's marriage with Bothwell, and, as we have seen, in that he was sincerely devoted to the Queen's interests. If, therefore, he concealed the secret of the forgery, or allowed Morton falsely to declare that he was present at the opening of the casket on the 21st June, his conduct was simply that of a mean and craven dastard,—a dastard, moreover, so paralyzed by selfish fear, that his marvellous penetration and shrewdness altogether deserted him. The theory that the letters were a forgery can therefore be maintained by Mr. Skelton, only on condition that he revokes every favourable estimate he has formed of Maitland; and *vice versa*, the acceptance of the genuineness of the letters seems to be the chief thing wanting to establish Mr. Skelton's theory of Maitland's high-minded consistency. Deny the genuineness of the letters, and Maitland's conduct becomes inexplicable on any theory that allows him even a shred of honesty or ability; but admit their genuineness, and most of the weak and inconsistent touches are removed from the striking historical portrait which in many other respects Mr. Skelton has limned with careful and felicitous skill.

One conclusion, therefore, established beyond all doubt by the tenor of Morton's declaration is, that the documents in the casket were "sichted" on the 21st June. This at once disposes of the very strong objection that has been taken to Moray's receipt of the 16th September 1568, testifying in the name of the Privy Council that Morton had " truly and honestly kept the said box," etc. " But here," says Goodall, " it comes naturally to be questioned how Murray, or his council, and especially he himself, who was in France at the time, could so readily and roundly attest, either that this box and letters were found with Dalgleish, or that Morton had so honestly preserved them all that time, without any manner of change or alteration? This seems repugnant to common sense, and is so far from answering their purpose, that it affords the most vehement presumption of fraud."[1] This opinion has been echoed and emphasized by many subsequent writers, and by none with more impressive and pungent reiteration than by Mr. Skelton. " They remained," he caustically observes, " for another year in the custody of the precise and scrupulous Morton" (ii. 279). " What was taken from the casket, what was placed in the casket, by Morton," he declares, " only Morton could tell; and Morton could keep his own counsel better than most men" (ii. 308). " Seeing that the casket," he further argues, " had been in Morton's custody for nearly fifteen months, it is hard to understand how Moray, untouched by any sense of shame, could have emitted such a declaration" (ii. 313). He even represents the case as an illustration of the maxim, " He who excuses, accuses himself;" for, says he, " Moray's assurance that the box had not been tampered with since it was

[1] Goodall, i. 41.

recovered, is calculated — for how could Moray know? — to intensify the suspicions it was meant to allay" (*ib.*).

Whatever force there may have been in such aphorisms previous to the discovery of Morton's declaration, it is indisputable that that declaration robs them of all their significance and sting. Not only so, but if the thesis of forgery is to be maintained, the whole chain of argument against the genuineness of the documents must be constructed anew from the very beginning. If the forgery was completed by the 20th June,—or only six days after Mary's surrender at Carberry Hill,—not only was it impossible for Crawford's declaration to be supplied to the forgers, but we must premise an almost superhuman promptness both of purpose and execution, to admit the possibility of manufacturing them out of "the mass of Mary's manuscripts found at Holyrood"—even supposing such a "mass" had been found—within such a limited time. To maintain the hypothesis of forgery, we are thus compelled to remove the date of the occurrence back to a period even anterior to Mary's capture at Carberry. The idea of a forgery, completed at such an early date, can scarcely be seriously entertained by even the most prejudiced defender of the Queen; and its probability does not, therefore, require any discussion

CHAPTER VIII.

CONCLUSION.

ONE of the circumstances that has been regarded as most strongly corroborative of the genuineness of the Casket Documents is the almost unbroken silence in reference to them maintained by Mary and her friends. When the silence was broken by Mary, it was under the compulsion of stern necessity, and the language made use of was indecisive and ambiguous. All that she instructed her Commissioners to say was: "I never writ anything concerning that matter to any creature; and gif ony sic writings be they are false and feinzeit forgit and invent be thamselfis, onlye to my dishonour and sclander; And thair ar divers in Scotland baith men and women, that can counterfeit my handwriting, and write the like maner of writing quhilk I use, as weill as myself, and principallie sic as ar in companie with thameselfis." This denial, such as it is, is deprived of all validity by the fact that Mary denied much more emphatically her authorship of the letters to Babington, the genuineness of which has now been conclusively established.

The denial is, however, a mere formal device, which probably did not deceive even her Commissioners, and amounts to little more than a transparent quibble. Her defenders denied, and she also would have denied, that the letters produced at Westminster contained any clear or direct reference to the murder. She never denied that while the conspiracy was in progress she wrote letters to Bothwell, nor did she deny that she signed the marriage contract of the 6th April, which was declared to be in the handwriting of Huntly. This omission, and the omission also of Huntly to deny the genuineness of the contract, are the more remarkable when it is remembered that she induced Huntly and Argyll to sign a statement implicating, so far as possible, the Earl of Moray in the plot against Darnley. Nor did the asserted confession of Bothwell, which formally declared that Mary was innocent of the murder, contain any denial that such letters were received by him from Mary. The confession is supposed to have been fabricated by the friends of the Queen, but whether fabricated or not, its silence in reference to the letters is equally significant. When the letters were published to the world in 1571 and 1572, Mary's silence regarding them, and the silence of her friends, remained practically unbroken. She had long had in her possession a version of the letters, and a copy of Buchanan's *Detectio* was sent her—undoubtedly with very bad taste—by Elizabeth. She bitterly, and perhaps with some justice, denounced in general terms the calumnious statements of the book, but remained silent in regard to the letters. Had they been founded on scraps of her own writing, had any of the letters been written by her to another than Bothwell, had they formed portions of a diary, or been compiled from her stray and isolated memoranda, she would have detected this, and have thus supplied the clue by which the forgery might easily have been exposed.

The apathy and caution of her friends, both in Scotland and on the Continent, in reference to the letters, is equally remarkable. The theory of forgery may have been hinted at, but it was never distinctly raised, nor was a proposal ever mooted by any of the great Catholic powers to have their genuineness tested. In like manner an ominous silence is maintained regarding them, not only in Mary's most confidential correspondence, but in the whole diplomatic correspondence of this period between the sovereigns of France and Spain and their ambassadors at foreign courts. To these sovereigns Mary appears to have made no direct appeal, or even any definite statement, in reference to the letters; and, while they appear to have given no instructions to their ambassadors to make inquiries in regard to such a very vital matter, none of these ambassadors report any definite opinion regarding them.

If the letters were forgeries, the Catholics come

almost as badly out of the affair as the Protestants, if not even worse than they; for Mary, with all her faults, deserved at least to be condemned, if she was to be condemned at all, on true and sufficient evidence; and it is in any case clear that her enemies had stronger objections to her Catholicism than to her murder of Darnley. On the supposition, however, that the letters are genuine, the conduct of the Catholics needs no explanation or apology, and they come certainly better out of the affair than the Protestants. They, at least, as a party, were not in any degree responsible for the murder of Darnley, but the same thing can scarcely be affirmed of the Protestants. It is impossible here to enter into a full consideration of the relation of the Earls of Moray and Morton, as well as other leading Protestant nobles, to the murder of Darnley; but it may safely be affirmed that their passive attitude during the progress of the plot can hardly be attributed to entire ignorance that it was in progress; and that their conduct can only be excused from a consideration of the difficulty and peril of their position after Mary's escape from Holyrood. They out-manœuvred Bothwell and Mary, and either suffered, or indirectly enticed them to commit the crime which occasioned their perdition. All that can be pled for them is, that they were not in a position to control the conduct of Mary or Bothwell, or to be held responsible for the misdeeds on which both were bent. Nor could they deem themselves called upon to endanger their own lives by seeking to preserve the worthless life of Darnley, whose betrayal of their former plans had cost them so dear. If Mary wrote the Casket Letters to Bothwell, she had become hopelessly incorrigible; and it cannot be affirmed that Moray, knowing his sister as he did, was acting either before or after the murder from motives of mere self-interest. Moray's estrangement from his sister dates from her marriage to Darnley. With that marriage also began her long series of misfortunes. They were partly due to Darnley's hopeless baseness and perversity. At any rate, so far as Moray was concerned in them, they are traceable rather to the absence of his guiding hand in directing his sister's policy than to the success of his direct efforts to subvert her authority.

As regards Elizabeth, the question of the genuineness of the letters necessarily greatly affects the judgment to be passed upon her treatment of the Queen of Scots. Elizabeth's position—whether she believed the letters to be genuine or not—was one of enormous perplexity. She was placed in a cruel dilemma. It was dangerous to be severe, and yet the temptation to use severity was peculiarly strong. Mary was perhaps the most deadly enemy she possessed. She had awakened Elizabeth's ill-will not merely by laying claim to the English throne, but by the fame of her remarkable personal charms. As the only great Protestant sovereign in Europe,

Elizabeth's position was specially perilous. Though Elizabeth had known the letters to be forgeries, she might have been excused for declining to aid her rival or to set her free; but indelible infamy would attach to the promulgation of such a vile calumny against her if it were baseless. On the other hand, if they were genuine, or if Elizabeth believed them to be so, it is difficult to discover any fault of a heinous kind in her treatment of Mary. Elizabeth's conduct was, perhaps, not consistent with strict rules of law or of equity,—superficially it was marked by hesitation, uncertainty, and fickleness,—but, nevertheless, if the letters were genuine, not only was it characterized by a regard to broad principles of justice, but by considerable long-suffering towards her unhappy captive, and by some merciful consideration for her, if not as a woman, at least as a deposed fellow-sovereign.

APPENDICES.

APPENDIX A.

---o---

THE EARL OF MORTON'S DECLARATION.

(From Folio 216 of No. 32,091 of the Additional MSS.
in the British Museum.)

> The trew declaration and Report of me
> James Erll of Mortoun how a certaine
> silver box owrgilt [1] conteyning dyvers   [1] overgilt.
> missive writtinges sonettz cõtractes and
> obligations for marriage betwix the
> Q. mother to our soveran lord, and
> James sometyme Erll bothwell wes
> found & usit.

Vpon thewrsday the xix of Junii 1567 I dynit at Ed^r.[2] [2] Edinburgh.
The L. of Ledingtoun secretarie w^t me. At tyme of my
dẽner a certaine man came to me. And in secrete mãner
schew me that thre servants of the Erll bothwills viz—
Mr Thomas hebburn persoun [3] of Auldhamesokkes, John [3] parson.
Cocburn brother to ye Lord of Stirling, and George
Dalgleische wer cũming to the toun, and passit win^t [4] [4] into.
the castell. Vpon q^{ch} adverteisment I on the suddane

send my cousing Mr And. Douglas & Robert Duglass his brother and James Johnstoun of Westerrall w^t others my servants to ye number of xvi or y^bu[1] toward ye castell & mak serche for the saidis psons[2] and gif possible wer to apprehend theme. According to q^ch my directioun, my servants past. And at ye firste missing ye fornamet thre psons for that yai was Deptit[3] furth of ye castell befor yair cũminge, my men then pting[4] in severall cumpaneis vpon knowledge that ye othoris quhom they socht wer separat, Mr And. Duglas socht for Mr Tho hebburn and fand him not, but gat his hors, James Johnstoun so^t for Jo Coeburg and apprehendit him, Robert Douglas suiting[5] for George Dalglesch efter he haid almast geven our his serche and inquisition. A gude fallow vnderstanding his purpose came to him offerand[6] for a meane pece of money to revele q^r[7] George dallgleis wes, The same w^t satisfeing him that gave ye intelligens for his pains, past to the potterraw befor Ed^r and there apprehendit ye said George with divers evidences & Lrts[8] in parchement, viz—the Erll bothwills infestmentes of Liddisdaill, of ye Lordshipp of Dunbarre & of Orknay & divers coy^ris q^ch all w^t the said George him self, the said robert bro^t and prentis[9] to me, And ye said George being examinat of ye caus of his Direction to ye castell of Ed^h and q^ch Lrts & evidences be bro^t fur^t of ye same alleget he was sent onlie to visit[10] etc L. bothwell his M^trs clething & that he had not ony Lrts nor cõmdetes[11] nor they q^ch wer apprehendit wth him, but his report being found suspicious and his gesture & behavio^r ministring cause of mistrust seing ye gravite of the actioun that wes in hand yt wes resolvit be cõmoun assent of ye Noble men cõvenit that ye said George

[1] thereabout.
[2] persons.
[3] departed.
[4] parting.
[5] seeking.
[6] offering.
[7] where.
[8] Letters.
[9] presents.
[10] inspect (French, visiter).
[11] commodities.

APPENDIX A. 115

Dalgleish suld be surelie kept that ny⁶,¹ And upon ¹ night.
the morn suld be haid to ye tolbuieth of Edinburgh and
yair be put in the payne and tormentid for furtheringe
of ye Declaration of ye trew^th q^ch being set upon friday
ye xx day of ye same moneth of Juini before any rigorous
Demaing² of his pson seing ye pane and movit of con- ² demeaning.
science, he callid for my cousing Mr And. Douglass qu^h a
c̃ũing³ ye said George desirit that ro^t douglass suld be ³ coming.
sent w^t him and he suld schaw & bring to licht that q^ch
he had. Sine being taken furth from ye payne, he past
w^t ye said ro^t to ye potteraw, And yare vnder the sceit of
a bedde tuke furth the said silver box q^ch he hade bro^t
furth of ye castell ye day before lokkit, and bro^t ye same
to me at viii hours at ny^t. And becaus it wes lait I
kepit it all that ny^t Vpon the morn viz setterday the
xxi of Juini in p̃ns⁴ of the Erlles of Atholl Marre Glen- ⁴ presence.
cairn myself, The LL Home, Sempill Sanquhar, The
M^r of Grahame & the Secretarie & Laird of tullibarden
comtrollar and ye said Mr And. Duglas the said box wes

stricken up becaus we wantid ye key, and ye L^tres⁵ win ⁵ Letters.
c̃otenit sichtit and Immediatlie therafter Delyverit agene
in my handis & custodie. Sen q^ch tyme I have observit
& kepit ye same box And all lres missives c̃otractes
sonettes and vy^ris writtes c̃otenit y^rin surelie w^tout alteration changeing eking⁶ or Dimissing⁷ of any thing found ⁶ increasing.
or ressavit in the said box   ⁷ diminish-
                                                             ing.

This I testify & declare to be vndowtid trew^th

This is ye copie of that q^ch was geven to M^r
Secretarie Cecill vpon Thursday the viii^th of Decem^b
1568

This is the trew copie of the Declaration maid &

presentit be the Erll of Mortoun to the Comissioners and cunsall of England sittand in Westminster for the tyme Vpon Thursday being the 29 of December 1568

  Sutcb wth his hand thus

         Mortoun.

APPENDIX B.

―o―

DEPOSITION OF LORD HOME AND KIRKALDY REGARDING THE CAUSE OF THEIR DEFECTION FROM THE PARTY OF KING JAMES VI.

(*a*) DEPOSITION OF LORD HOME, 31ST JULY 1573.

(From Folio 270 of No. 32,091 of the Additional MSS. in the British Museum.)

> In the castell of Edinburg the last day of Julij The yeir of Imv^{c}Lxxiij (1573) yeirs In presence of Allane Lord Cathcart Sr Johnne bellenden of auchnoule knight, Justice clerk Maister James Halyburtoun provost of Dundie and george dowglas of parkheid cap^{ne} of the said castell of Ed^r

ALEXANDER sumtyme lord hwme being examinat and inquirit wes the occassioun of his defectioun from the kingis Maiesties obedience. Declared that efter the taking of umqle William Maitland sumtyme of Lethingtoun younger, secretare for the tyme. This deponer wrait a lre to my lord of Murray then Regent quhairw^th he can not Juge bot the Regent wes offendit, yit thairefter he come to this deponers house of hwme and tareit a night at ylk tyme this deponer belevis that all occasioun of misliking betuix thame wes removed, And efter that this deponer come to the secretares day of law, to assist his frend (as he sayis) according to the custume of scotland, and nevirtheles spak wth the Regent and did his dewetie to him before this deponer departit out of Ed^r.

Denyis that evir he maid defection from the kingis obedience in the lyvetime of my lord of Murray Regent.

Inquirit gif the occasion of his defectioun from the kingis service wes becaus that he being desirit be umqle the erll of Murray regent for the tyme to have bene partaker wth him of the death and distructioun of the king o^r soveraine lord that now is, to mak the erll of Murray him self king. And that this deponer refusit to consent thairto, as hes bene bruitit and sett out in print and utherwise divulgat to the warld. This deponer vpoun his saule faith houno^r and trewth declaris That he wes nevir desirit to have bene powtaker wth the said vmqle lord Regent of the death and distructioun of o^r said soveraine lord that now is to mak the said erll of Murray king as is above requirit. Nor nevir hard of ony sic motioun devise purpois or intentioun. Bot thinkis that quhasaevir hes maid or sett out ony sic report to the warld in speche writt or print hes abusit this deponers name and spokin and writtin agains the trewth. And that the verie occasioun of his defectioun (as he affirms) wes the skaith he sustenit of england; for seking redres quhairof he wes glaid to seik sic freindes and help as he culd find

  (signed) J. Bellenden
       Allan Lord Cathcart
       James Halyburton
       George Douglas of Parkheid
       Alexander Home
           J. Hay (clerk).

(*b*) Deposition of William Kirkaldy of Grange, 3rd August 1573.

(From Folio 272 of No. 32,091 of the Additional MSS. in the British Museum.)

At halyrudehous the third day of august the yeir of God I.mv^c thre score threttene yeirs (1573) In presence of Robert Lord boyd Sr Johanne bellenden of Auchnoule Knight Justice clerk and Maister James Lawsoun minister of the kirk of Ed^r

William Kirkcaldy sumtyme of Grange Kng^t being examinat and inquirit gif the occasioun of his defectioun from the kingis service wes Because that he being requirit be vmq^{le} the erll of Murray regent for the tyme, to have bene partaker wth him of the death and distructioun of the king o^r soveraine lord that now is To mak the erll of

Murray him self king. And that this deponar refusit to assent thairto. As hes bene bruitit and sett out in print and otherwys divulgit to the warld.

This deponair vpoun his saule fayth and trewth declaris and testifiis that he wes nevir desirit or requirit be ye said erll of Murray to have bene partaker wth him of o^r said soveraine lordis Death and distructioun To mak the said erll of Murray king as is before specifit. Nor nevir hard of ony sic motioun devise purpos or intentioun. And thairfore quhasaevir hes maid or sett out ony sic report to the Warld in speche write or print hes Done this Deponer Iniurie, abusit his Name and spokin and writtin agains the trewth. And finallie declaris that he knew nevir of ony sic vngodllie and tressonable devyse or intentioun to haif bene thocht or proponit be ye said vmq^{le} erle of murray in his lyvetyme. Nor nevir hard of the buke sett out on this mater q^{ll} now that it is presently declarit vnto him

R. boyd. W. Kyrkcaldy. J. Bellondon. M. James Lawsone minister of ye kirk of Edinburghe

APPENDIX C.

CASKET DOCUMENTS.

Marriage Contracts.

THE FIRST CONTRACT.

Nous Marie, par la grace de Dieu, Royne d'Escosse, douaryere de France, &c. promettons fidellement & de bonne foy, & sans contraynte, à Jaques Hepburn conte de Boduel, de n'avoir jamays autre espoulx & mary que luy, & de le prendre pour tel toute & quant fois qu'il m'en requerira, quoy que parents, amys ou autres, y soient contrayres. Et puis que Dieu a pris mon feu mary Henry Stuart dit Darnlay, & que par ce moien je sois libre, n'estant soubs obeissance de pere, ni de mere, des mayntenant je proteste que, lui estant en mesme liberté, je seray preste, & d'accomplir les ceremonies requises au mariage : que je lui promets devant Dieu, que j'en prantz à tesmoignasge, & la presente, signeé de ma mayn : ecrit ce——

MARIE R.

THE SECOND CONTRACT.

At Setoun, the v. day of April, the zeir of God 1567, the richt excellent, richt heich and michtie Princes Marie, be the Grace of God, Quene of Scottis, considering the place and estait quhairin Almightie God hes constitute hir heichnes, and how, be the deceis of the king hir husband, hir Majestie is now destitute of ane Husband, leving solitaire in the stait of wedowheid: In the quhilk kynde of lyfe hir Majestie maist willingly wald continew, gif ye weill of hir realme and subjectis wald permit: Bot on the uther part, considering the inconveniencis may follow, and the necessitie quhilk the realme hes, yat hir Majestie be couplit with ane husband, hir Heichness hes inclynit to mary. And seing quhat incommoditie may cum to this realme, in case hir Majestie suld joyne in mariage with ony forane Prince of ane strange natioun, hir Heichnes hes thocht rather better to zeild unto ane of hir awin subjectis: Amangis quhome hir Majestie findis nane mair abill, nor indewit with better qualities then the richt nobill and hir deir cousin, James Erle Bothwell, &c. of quhais thankfull and trew service hir Heichnes, in all tymes bypast, hes had large prufe and infallibill experience. And seing not only the same gude mynd constantly persevering in him, bot with that ane inward affection and hartly lufe towardis hir Majestie, hir Heichness, amangis the rest, hes maid hir chose of him: And thairfoir, in the presence of the eternall God, faithfully, and in the word of ane Prince, be thir presentis, takis the said James Erle Bothwell as hir lawfull husband, and promittis and oblissis hir

Heichnes, that howsone the proces of divorce, intentit betwixt ye said Erle Bothwell and Dame Jane Gordoun, now his pretensit spous, beis endit be the ordour of ye lawis, hir Majestie sall, God willing, thairefter schortly mary and tak the said Erle to hir husband, and compleit the band of matrimonie with him, in face of holy kirk, and sall never mary nane uther husband bot he only, during his lyfetyme. And as hir Majestie, of hir gratious humanitie and proper motive, without deserving of the said Erle, hes thus inclynit hir favour and affection towardis him, he humblie and reverentlie acknowledging the same according to his bound dewtie, and being als fré and abill to mak promeis of mariage, in respect of the said proces of divorce, intentit for divers ressonabill causis, and that his said pretensit spous hes thairunto consentit, he presentlie takis hir Majestie as his lauchfull spous in the presence of God, and promittis and oblissis him, as he will answer to God, and upon his fidelitie and honour, that, in all diligence possibill, he sall prosecute and set fordward the said proces of divorce alreddy begunne and intentit betwix him and the said Dame Jane Gordoun his pretensit spous, unto the fynal end of ane decrett and declarator thairin. And incontinent thairefter, at hir Majesteis gude will and plesure, and quhen hir Heichness thinkis convenient, sall compleit and solemnizat, in face of haly kirk, ye said band of matrimony with hir Majestie and lufe, honour and serve hir Heichness, according to the place and honour that it hes pleisit hir Majestie to accept him unto, and never to have ony uther for his wyfe, during hir Majesteis lyfetime: In faith and witnessing quhairof, hir Heichness and the said Erle hes subscrivit this present faithfull promeis with yair handis, as followis, day, zeir and place foirsaidis, befoir thir witnesses George Erle of Huntly, and Maister Thomas Hepburne Persoun of Auldhamstock &. Sic subsributur

Marie R.
James Erle Bothwell.

THE CASKET LETTERS.

Letter I.

(a) Published Scotch Translation.

It appeiris, that with zour absence thair is alswa joynit forgetfulnes, seand yat at zour departing ze promysit to mak me advertisement of zour newis from tyme to tyme. The waitting upon yame zesterday causit me to be almaist in sic joy as I will be at zour returning, quhilk ze have delayit langer than zour promeis was.

As to me, howbeit I have na farther newis from zow, according to my comissioun, I bring the Man with me to Craigmillar upon Monounday quhair he will be all Wednisday; and I will gang to Edinburgh to draw blude of me,

(b) English Translation at the Record Office.

(State Papers relating to Mary Queen of Scots, vol. ii. No. 66.)

It seemyth that with your absence forgetfulness is joynid consydering that at your departure you promised me to send me newes from you. Nevertheless I can learn none. And yet did I yesterday looke for that that shuld make me meryer than I shall be. I think you doo the lyke for your return, prolonging it more than you have promised.

As for me, if I hear no other matter of you, according to my commission, I bring the man Monday to Cregmillar, where he shall be upon Wednisday. And I go to Edinborough to be lett blud, if I hear no word to the contrary.

gif in the meane tyme I get na newis in ye contrary fra zow.

He is mair gay than ever ze saw him; he puttis me in remembrance of all thingis yat may mak me beleve he luifis me. Summa, ze will say yat he makis lufe to me: of ye quhilk I tak sa greit plesure, yat I enter never where he is, but incontinent I tak ye seiknes of my sair syde, I am sa troubillt with it. Gif Paris bringis me that quhilk I send him for, I traist it sall amend me.

I pray zow, advertise me of zour newis at lenth, and quhat I sall do in cace ze be not returnit quhen I am cum thair; for, in cace ze wirk not wysely, I sé that the haill burding of this will fall upon my schoulderis. Provide for all thing, and discourse upon it first with zourself. I send this be Betoun, quha gais to ane day of law of the Laird of Balfouris. I will say na further, saifing that I pray zow to send me gude newis of zour voyage. From Glasgow this Setterday in the morning.

He is the meryest that ever you sawe, and doth remember unto me all that he can, to make me believe that he loveth me. To conclude, you wold say that he maketh love to me, wherein I take so much pleasure, that I have never com in there, but the payne of my syde doth take me. I have it sore today. If Paris doth bring back unto me that for which I have sent, it suld much amend me.

I pray you, send me word from you at large, and what I shall doo if you be not returned, when I shall be there. For if you be not wyse I see assuredly all the wholle burden falling upon my shoulders. Provide for all and consyder well first of all. I send this present to Ledington to be delivered to you by Beton, who goeth to one day a law of Lor Balfour. I will say no more unto you, but that I pray God send me goode newes of your voyage.

From Glasco this Saturday morning.[1]

(c) Published Latin Translation.

Videtur, cum tua absentia conjuncta esse obliviscentia, praesertim cùm in tuo discessu pro-

(d) Published French Translation.

Il semble, q'avec vostre absence soit joinct l'oubly, veu qu'au partir vous me promistes de vos

---

[1] This letter is endorsed in the hand of a clerk, "Ane short lettre from Glasco to the Erle of Bothwell; profs her disdayn again her husband." Cecil' mark is added below.

miseris, quòd me certiorem faceres, si quid incidisset tibi novi, per singula propè momenta. Eorum exspectatio propemodum in tantam laetitiam me conjecit, quam in tuo reditu sim acceptura, quem distulisti ultrà quàm promiseras.

Quod ad me attinet, quanquam mihi audiam praeterea ex te novi, tamen juxta partes mihi commissas, hominem adduco mecum ad Cragmillarium die lunae, ubi erit toto die Mercurii; ego autem ibo Edinburgum, ut mittam ex me sanguinem, si nihil interea novi in contrarium de te audiam.

Est hilarior, ac vegetior, quàm unquam eum videris; subjicit mihi in memoriam omnia, quae efficere queant ut me credam ab eo amari. In summa diceres quòd me cum summa observantia colat & ambiat; qua de re ita magnam capio voluptatem, quòd nunquam ad eum ingredior, quin dolor lateris mei infirmi me invadat, ita me malè habet. Si Paris ad me asseret id, cujus causâ eum miseram, spero me meliùs habituram.

Oro, fac me certiorem de tuis rebus prolixè & quid mihi sit faciendum, si tu non eris reversus cùm ego illuc venero; quia nisi tu rem geras prudenter, video totum onus in meos humeros inclinaturam. Prospice omnia, ac priùs tecum rem expende. Haec tibi mitto per Betonem, qui proficiscitur ad diem dictum D. Balfurio. Non dicam plura, nisi quòd te rogo ut de tuo itinere me

nouvelles, & toutesfois je n'en puis apprendre; de quoy l'esperance m'a quasi jetté en aussi grande joye, que celle que Je doy recevoir à vostre venue, laquelle vous avez differée plus que ne m'aviez promis.

Quant à moy, encor que Je n'oye rien de nouveau de vous, toutesfois, selon la charge que J'ay receuë, j'ameine l'homme avec moy Lundy à Cragmillar, où il sera tout le Mecredy; & j'iray á Edimbourg pour me faire tirer du sang, si je n'enten rien de nouveau de vous au contraire.

Il est plus joyeux & dispos, que vous ne l'avez jamais veu; il me reduict en memoire toutes les choses qui me peuvent faire entendre qu'il m'aime. En somme vous diriez, qu'il m'honnore, & recherche avec grand respect: en quoy Je pren si grand plaisir, que Je n'entre jamais vers luy, que la douleur de mon costé malade ne me saisisse, tant il me fasche. Si Paris m'apportoit ce pourquoy j'avoye envoyé, j'espere que je me porteroye mieux.

Je vous prie, faictes moy sçavoir bien au long de vos affaires, & ce qu'il me faut faire, si vous n'estes de retour quand je seray là arrivée; car si vous ne conduisez la chose sagement, je voy que tout le faix retournera sur mes espaules. Regardez à tout, & premierement espluchez le faict en vous-mesmes. Je vous envoye ceci par Beton, qui s'en ira au jour assigné au Sieur Balfurd. Je ne vous en

APPENDIX C.

certiorem facias. Glascua hoc Sabbato manè. diray d'avantage, sinon pour vous prier que me faciez entendre de vostre voyage. A Glascwo ce Samedy matin.

Letter II.

(c) Published Scotch Translation.

Being departit from the place quhair I left my hart, it is esie to be judgeit quhat was my countenance, seeing that I was evin als mekle as ane body without ane hart; quhilk was the Occasioun that quhile Denner tyme I held purpois to na body; nor zit durst ony present thamselfis unto me, judging yat it was not gude sa to do.

Four myle or I came to the towne, ane gentilman of the Erle of Lennox came and maid his commendatiounis unto me; and excusit him that he came not to meit me, be ressoun he durst not interpryse the same, becaus of the rude wordis that I had spokin to Cuninghame: And he desyrit that he suld come to the inquisitioun of ye matter yat I suspectit him of. This last speiking was of his awin heid, without ony commissioun.

I answerit to him that thair was na receipt culd serve aganis feir; and that he wold not be affrayit, in cace he wer not culpabill; and that I answerit hot rudely to the doutis yat wer in his letteris. Summa, I maid him hald his toung. The rest

(d) English Translation.

(State Papers, Mary Queen of Scots, vol. ii. No. 65.)

Being gon from the place, where I had left my harte, it may be easily judged what my countenance was consydering what the body without harte, whilk was cause that till dynner I had used lyttle talk, neyther wold anybody venture

ad~~vance~~ himselfe thereunto, thinking that it was not good so to do.

Four myles from thence a gentleman of the Erle of Lennox cam and made his commendations and excuses unto me, that he cam not to meet me, because he durst not enterprise so to do, considering the sharp words that I had spoken to Conyngham, and that he desired that I wold come to the inquisition of the facts which I did suspect him of. This last was of his own head, without commission, and I told him that he had no receipt against aganist feare, and that he had no fear, if he did not feele himself faulty, and that I had also sharply answered to the doubts that he made in his letters as though there had been a meaning to pursue him. To be short I have made him hold his peace; for the rest it were too long to tell

were lang to wryte. Schir James
Hamiltoun met me, quha schawit
that the uther tyme quhan he
hard of my cumming, he departit
away, and send Howstoun, to
schaw him, that he wald never
have belevit that he wald have
persewit him, nor zit accompanyit
him with the Hamiltounis. He
answerit, that he was only cum
bot to see me, and yat he wald
nouther accompany Stewart nor
Hammiltoun, bot be my com-
maundement. He desyrit that he
wald cum and speik with him:
He refusit it.

The Laird of Lusse, Howstoun,
and Caldwellis sone, with xl.
hors or thairabout, came and met
me. The Laird of Lusse said, he
was chargeit to ane day of law be
the King's father, quhilk suld be
this day, aganis his awin hand-
writ, quhilk he hes : and zit notwithstanding, knawing of my
cumming, it is delayit. He was
inquyrit to cum to him, quhilk he
refusit, and sweiris that he will
indure nathing of him. Never
ane of that towne came to speik
to me, quhilk causis me think
that they ar his; and neuertheles
he speikis gude, at the leist his
sone. I se na uther Gentilman
bot thay of my company.

The King send for Joachim
yesternicht,[1] and askit at him,
quhy I ludgeit not besyde him?
And that he wald ryse the soner
gif that wer: and quhairfoir I
come, gif it was for gude appoint-
ment? and gif I had maid my

you. Sir James Hamilton came
to meet me, who told me that at
another tyme he went his way
when he heard of my comming,
and that he sent unto him Hous-
town, to tell him that he wold not
have thought, that he wold have
followed and accompany himself
with the Hamiltons. He answered
that he was not come but to see
me; and that he would not follow
Stuart nor Hamilton, but by my
commandment. He prayed him
to go speak to him; he refuses it.

The Lord Luce, Houstoun and
the sonne of Caldwell, and about
XLty horse came to meet me that
he was sent to one day o' law from
the father, which shold be this
day against the signing of his own
hand, which he has, and that,
knowing of my comming, he hath
delayed it, and hath prayed him
to go see him, which he hath
refused and give aith that he
will suffer nothing at his hands.
Not one of the town is come to
~~to see me~~
speak with me, which makith me
to think that they be his, and
they so speakith well of them at
least his sonne.

The King sent for Joachim and
asked him, why I did not lodge
nigh to him, and that he wold
ryse sooner and why I came,
whithir it wear for any good ap-
pointment, that he came, and
whithir I had not taken Paris

---

[1] Yesternight, it will be observed, does not occur in the English version.

APPENDIX C.   129

estait, gif I had takin Paris,* and Gilbert to wryte to me? And yat I wald send Joseph away. I am abaschit quha hes schawin him sa far; zea he spak evin of ye marriage of Bastiane. I inquyrit him of his letteris, quhairintil he plenzeit of the crueltie of sum: answerit, that he was astonischit, and that he was sa glaid to sé me, that he belevit to die for glaidness. He fand greit fault that I was pensive.

I departit to supper. This beirer will tell yow of my arryuing. He prayit me to returne: the quhilk I did. He declairit unto me his seiknes, and that he wald mak na testament, bot only leif all thing to me; and that I was the cause of his maladie, becaus of the regrait that he had that I was sa strange unto him.² And thus he said: Ze ask me quhat I mene be the crueltie contenit in my letter? it is of zow alone that will not accept my offeris and repentance. I confess that I haue failit, bot not into that qubilk I ever denyit; and sicklyke hes failit to sindrie of zour subjectis, quhilk ze haue forgeuin.

I am young.

Ze wil say, that ze have forgevin me oft tymes, and zit yat I returne to my faultis. May not

and Guilbert to write and that I sent Joseph. I wonder who hath told him so much even of the marriage of Bastian. This bearer shall tell you more upon that I asket him of his letters and where he did complayn of the cruelty of some of them. He said that he did dreme, and that he was so glad to see me that he thought he should dye. Indeed that he has found fault with me.

I went my way to supp. This bearer shall tell you of my arryving. He praied me to come agayn, which I did: and he told me his grefe, and that he wold make no testament, but leave all unto me and that I was cause of his sickness for the sorrow he had, that I was so strange unto him.² "And (said he) you asked what I ment in my letter to speak of cruelty. It was of your cruelty who will not accept my offres and repentance I avow that I have done amisse, but not that I have also always disavoued; and so have many othir of your subjects don and you have well pardoned them.

I am young.

You will say that you have also pardoned me in my time and that I returne to my fault. May not

* this berer will tell you somwhat upon this.¹

---
¹ Apparently a note on the margin of the original letter.
² The succeeding portion of the letter corresponds closely with Crawford's declaration, which is here quoted:—"And moreover he saide, Ye asked me what I ment bye the crueltye specified in mye lettres; yat procedethe of yow onelye, that wille not accepte mye offres and'repentance. I confesse that I have failed in som thingis, and yet greater faultes have bin made to yow sundrye times, which ye have forgiven. I am but yonge, and ye will saye ye have forgivne me diverse tymes. Maye not a man of mye age, for lack of counselle, of which I

ane man of my age, for lacke of counsell, fall twyse or thryse, or inlacke of his promeis, and at last repent himself, and be chastisit be experience? Gif I may obtene pardoun, I protest I sall never mak fault agane. And I craif na uther thing, bot yat we may be at bed and buird togidder as husband and wyfe; and gif ze will not consent heirunto, I sall never ryse out of yis bed. I pray zow, tell me your resolutioun. God knawis how I am puneschit for making my God of zow, and for hauing na uther thocht but on zow; and gif at ony tyme I offend zow, ze ar the caus, becaus, quhen ony offendis me, gif, for my refuge, I micht playne unto zow, I wald speik it unto na uther body; bot quhen I heir ony thing, not being familiar with zow, necessitie constrains me to keep it in my breist; and yat causes me to tyne my wit for verray anger.

I answerit ay unto him, but that wald be ovir lang to to wryte at lenth. I askit quhy he wald

a man of my age for want of counsel, faylle twise or thrise and mysse of promis and at the last repent and rebuke himself by his experience? If I may obtayn this pardon I protest I will not make fault agayn. And I ask nothing but that we may be at bed and table together as husband and wife; and if you will not I will never rise from this bed. I pray you tell me your resolution hereof. God knoweth that I am punished to have made my God of you and had no other mynd but of you. And when I offend you sometime, you are cause thereof: for if I thought, when anybody doth any wrong to me, that I might for my resource make my moan thereof unto you, I wold open it to no other, but when I heare anything being not familiar with you, I must keep it in my mynd and that ~~maketh me out of my wit~~ troublith my wit for anger.

I did still answer him but that I shall be too long. In the end I asked him whether he would go

am verye destitute, falle twise or thrise, and yet repent, and be chastised bye experience? Gif I have made anye faile that ye but thinke a faile, howe soever it be, I crave your pardone, and proteste that I shall never faile againe. I desire no other thinge but that we maye be together as husband and wife. And if ye will not consent hereto, I desire never to rise forthe of this bed. Therefore, I praye yow, give me an aunswer hereunto. God knoweth howe I am punished for making mye god of yow, and for having no other thought but on yow. And if at anie tyme I offend yow, ye are the cause; for that when aine offendethe me, if for my refuge I might open mye minde to yow, I woulde speake to no other; but when anie thinge is spoken to me, and ye and I not beinge as husband and wife ought to be, necessitie compelleth me to kepe it in my brest, and bringethe me in such melancolye as ye see me in. She aunswered, that it semed hym she was sorye for his sicknesse, and she woulde find remedye therefore so sone as she might."

pas away in ye *Inglis* schip. He denyis it, and sweiris thairunto; bot he grantis that he spak with the men. Efter this I inquyrit him of the inquisitioun of Hiegait. He denyit the same, quhill I schew him the verray wordis was spokin. At quhilk tyme he said, that Mynto had advertisit him, that it was said, that sum of the counsell had brocht an letter to me to be subscrivit to put him in Presoun, and to slay him gif he maid resistance. And he askit the same at Mynto himself; quha answerit, that he belevit ye same to be trew. The morne I wil speik to him upon this Point. As to the rest of Willie Hiegait's, he confessit it, bot it was the morne efter my cumming or he did it.

He would verray fane that I suld ludge in his ludgeing. I refusit it, and said to him, that he behovit to be purgeit, and that culd not be done heir. He said to me, I heir say ze have brocht ane lytter with zow; but I had rather have passit with zow. I trow he belevit that I wald have send him away Presoner. I answerit, that I wald tak him with me to Craigmillar, quhair the mediciner and I micht help him, and not be far from my sone. He answerit, that he was reddy when I pleisit, sa I wald assure him of his requeist.

He desyris na body to se him. He is angrie quhen I speik of Walcar, and sayis, that he sall pluk the ciris out of his heid and that he leis: For I inquyrit him

in the English shipp. He doth disavow it and swearith so, and confessith to have spoken to the men. Afterwards I asked him of the inquisition of Hiegate. He denyed it till I told him the very words, that it was said, that som of the counsyle had brought me a letter to signe to putt him in prison, and to kill him if he did resist and that he asked this of Minto himself, who said unto him that he thought it was true. I will talke with him to morrow upon that poynte. The rest as Wille Hiegate hath confessed; but it was the next day that he came hither.

.

In the end he desyred much that I shuld lodge in his lodging. I have refused it. I have told him that he must be pourged and that could not be don heere. He said unto me "I have heard say that you have brought the lytter, but I wold rather have gon with yourself." I told him that so I wold myself bring him to Craigmillar, that the phisicians and I also might cure him without being farr from my sonn. He said that he was ready when I wold so as I wold assure him of his request.

He hath no desyre to be seen and waxeth angry when I speake to him of Wallear and saith that he will pluck his ears from his head, and that he lieth; for I

upon that, and yat he was angrie with sum of the Lordis, and wald threittin thame. He denyis that, and sayis he luifis thame all, and prayis me to give traist to nathing aganis him. As to me, he wald rather give his lyfe or he did ony displesure to me. And efter yis he schew me of sa money lytil flattereis, sa cauldly and sa wysely that ze will abasche thairat. I had almaist forzet that he said, he could not dout of me in yis purpois of Hiegaite's; for he wald never beleif yat I, quha was his proper flesche, wald do him ony evill; alsweill it was schawin that I refusit to subscribe the same; But as to ony utheris that wald persew him, at leist he suld sell his lyfe deir aneuch; but he suspectit na body, nor zit wald not; but wald lufe all yat I lufit.

He wald not let me depart from him, bot desyrit yat I suld walk with him. I mak it seme that I beleive that all is trew, and takis heid thairto, and excusit my self for this nicht that I culd not walk. He sayis, that he sleipis not weil. Ze saw him never better, nor speik mair humbler. And gif I had not ane prufe of his hart of waxe, and yat myne wer not of ane dyamont, quhairintill na schot can brek, but that quhilk cummis forth of zour hand, I wald have almaist had pietie of him. But feir not, the place sall hald unto the deith. Remember, in recompence thairof, that ye

asked him before of that, and what cause he had to complayn of some of the lords and to threaten them. He denyeth it, and saith that he had allready prayed them to think no such matter of him. As for myself he wold rather lose his lyfe than doo me the least displeasure; and then used so many kinds of flatteries so coldly and wysely as you wold marvayle at. I had forgotten that he sayde that he could not mistrust me for Hiegate's word, for he could not believe, that his own flesh (which was myself) wold doo him any hurte; and indeed it was sayd that I refused to have him let bludd.[1] But for the others he wold at least sell his lyfe deare ynoughe; but that he did suspect nobody nor wolde, but love all that I did love.

He wold not lett me go, but wold have me to watche with him. I made as though I thought all to be true and that I wold think upon it, and have excused myself from sytting up with him this nyght, for he saith that he sleepith not. You have never heard him speake better nor more humbly; and if I had not proof of his hart to be as waxe, and that myne were not as a dyamant, no stroke but comming from your hand wold make me but to have pitee of him. But fear not for the place shall continue till death. Remember also, in recompense thereof, not to suffer yours to be won by that

---

[1] The translator apparently mistook "signer" for "saigner."

suffer not zouris to be wyn be that fals race that will travell na less with zow for the same.

I beleve thay have bene at schullis togidder. He hes ever the teir in his eye; he salutis every body, zea, unto the leist, and makis picteous caressing unto thame, to mak thame have pictie on him. This day his father bled at the mouth and nose; ges quhat presage that is. I have not zit sene him, he keipis his chalmer. The king desyris that I suld give him meit with my awin handis; bot gif na mair traist quhair ze ar, than I sall do heir.

This is my first jornay: I sall end ye same ye morne. I wryte all thingis, howbeit thay be of lytill wecht, to the end that ze may tak the best of all to judge upon. I am in doing of ane work heir that I hait greitly. Have ze not desyre to lauch to sé me lie sa weill, at ye leist to dissembill sa weill, and to tell him treuth betwix handis? He schawit me almaist all yat is in the name of the Bischop and Sudderland, and zit I have never twichit ane word of that ze schawit me; but all-anerly be force, flattering, and to pray him to assure himself of me. And be pleinzeing on the Bischop, I have drawin it all out of him. Ye have hard the rest.

false race that wold do no less to yourself.

I think they have bene at school togither. He has allwais the tears in his eye. He saluteth every man, even to the meanest, and maketh much of them, that they may take pitie of him. His father has bled this day at the nose and at the mouth—gess what token that is. I have not seen him; he is in his chamber. The king is so desyrous, that I shuld give him meat with my own hands, but trust you no more there where you are than I doo here.

This is my first journay; I will end tomorrow. I write all, how little consequence so ever it be, to the end that you may take of the whole that shall be best *for you to judge*.[1] I do here a work that I hate much, *but I had begun it this morning;*[2] had you not lyst to laugh, to see me so trymly make a lie, at the least dissemble, and to mingle truthe therewith. He hath almost told me all on the bishops behalf and of Sunderland, without touching any word unto him of that which you had told me; but only by much flattering him and praying him, and by my complayning of the bishop, *I have taken the worms out* of his nose.[3] You have heard the rest.

---

[1] On the margin, "for your purpose."
[2] No equivalent in the Scotch version.
[3] Explained on the margin, "I have disclosed all—I have known what I wold." A similar phrase occurs in a genuine letter of Mary, 5th October 1568: "Il m'a voulu tirer les vers du nez et scavoir ma delue."—Labanoff, ii. 213.

We are couplit with twa fals races; the devil sinder us, and God knit us togidder for ever, for the maist faithful coupill that ever be unitit. This is my faith, I will die in it.

Excuse I wryte evill, ye may ges ye half of it; bot I cannot mend it, becaus I am not weil at eis; and zit verray glaid to wryte unto zow quhen the rest are sleipand, sen I cannot sleip as thay do, and as I wald desyre, that is in zour armes, my deir lufe, quhome I pray God to preserve from all evill, and send zow repois: I am gangand to seik myne till ye morne, quhen I sall end my Bybill; but I am faschit that it stoppis me to wryte newis of myself unto zow, because it is sa lang.

Advertise me quhat ze have deliberat to do in the mater ze knaw upon this point, to ye end that we may understand utheris weill, that nathing thairthrow be spilt.

I am irkit, and ganging to sleip, and zit I ceis not to scrible all this paper in sa mekle as restis thairof. Waryit not this pokische man be that causes me haif sa mekle pane, for without him I suld have an far plesander subject to discourse upon. He is not over mekle deformit, zit he hes ressavit verray mekle. He hes almaist slane me with his braith; it is worse than zour uncle's; and zit

We are tyed to by two false races. The *good yeere*[1] sunder us and God knytt us togither for ever for the most faythfull couple that ever he did knytt togither. This is my faith; I will dye in it.

Excuse it if I write ill; you must gesse the one halfe I cannot doo with all, for I am yll at case, and glad to write unto you when other folke be asleep, seeing that I cannot doo as they doo, according to my desyre, that is between your arms my dear lyfe whom I beseech God to preserve from all yll, and send you good rest as I go to seek myne, till tomorrow in the morning that will end my bible. But it greevith me, that it should lett me from wryting unto you of newes of myself, long the same.
so much I have to write

Send me word what you have determined here upon, that we may know the one the others mind for marring of any thing.

I am weary, and am asleepe, and yet I cannot forbear scribbling so long as there is any paper. Cursed be this pocky fellow that troublith me thus much, for I had a pleasanter matter to discourse unto you but for him. He is not much the worse, but he is yll arrayd.[2] I thought I shuld have been kylled with his breth, for it is worse than your uncle's breth; and yet I was sett no nearer to him

---

[1] In Scotch "devil." French in both instances possibly misread.
[2] French "rescu" misread as "vescu."

APPENDIX C. 135

I cam na neirer unto him, bot in ane chyre at the bed seit, and he being at the uther end thairof.

The message of the father in the gait.

The purpois of Schir James Hamilton.

Of that the Laird of Lusse schawit me of the delay

Of the demaudis that he askit at Joachim

Of my estait

Of my company

Of the occasioun of my cumming:

And of Joseph

Item, The purpois that he and I had togidder. Of the desyre that he hes to pleis me, and of his repenteuce.

Of the interpretatioun of his letter

Of Willie Hiegaite's mater of his departing.

Of Monsiure de Levingstoun

I had almaist forzet, that Monsiure de Levingstoun said in the Lady Reres eir at supper, that he wald drink to ye folk yat I wist of, gif I wald pledge thame. And efter supper he said to me, quhen I was lenand upon him warming me at the fyre, Ze have fair going to sé seik folk, zit ze cannot be sa welcum to thame as ze left sum body this day in regrait, that will never be blyth quhill he sé zow agane. I askit at him quha that was With that he thristit my body, and said, that sum of his folkis had sene than in a chayr by his bolster, and he lyeth at the further syde of the bed.

The message of the Father by the way

The talk of Sir James H̶a̶m̶i̶l̶t̶o̶n̶[1] of the ambassador

That the Lard of Luss hath told me of the delay

The questions that he asked of Jochim

Of my state

Of my company

And of the cause of my comming

And of Joseph

The talk that he and I had, and of his desyre to please me, of his repentance, and of the interpretation of his letter

Of Will Hiegate's doing, and of his departure, and of the L. of Livinston.

I had forgotten of the L. of Livinston, that he at supper sayd softly to me, when I was leaning upon him and warming myself. " You may well go and see sick folk, yet can you not be so welcome unto them as you have this day left somebody in payne " I asked him who it was; he took me about the body and said " One of his folke that has left you this day." Gesse you the rest.

---

[1] Hamilton struck out as printed.

zow in fascherie; ze may ges at the rest.

I wrocht this day quhill it was two houris upon this bracelet, for to put the key of it within the lock thairof, quhilk is couplit underneth with twa cordounis. I have had sa lytill tyme that it is evill made; bot I sall mak ane fairer in the meanetyme. Tak heid that nane that is heir sé it, for all the warld will knaw it, becaus for haist it was maid in yair presence.

I am now passand to my fascheous purpois. Ze gar me dissemble sa far, that I haif horring thairat; and ye caus me do almaist the office of a traitores. Remember how gif it wer not to obey zow, I had rather be deid or I did it; my hart bleidis at it. Summa, he will not cum with me, except upon conditioun that I will promeis to him, that I sall be at bed and buird with him as of befoir, and that I sall leif him na ofter: and doing this upon my word, he will do all thingis that I pleis, and cum with me. Bot he hes prayit me to remane upon him quhil uther morne.

He spak verray bravely at ye beginning, as yis beirer will schaw zow, upon the purpois of the Inglismen, and of his departing: Bot in ye end he returnit agane to his humilitie.

He schawit, amangis uther purposis, yat he knew weill aneuch that my brother had schawin me yat thing, quhilk he had spoken in Striviling, of the quhilk he

This day I have wrought till two of the clock upon this bracelet, to putt the key in the clifte of it, which is tyed with two laces. I have had so little tyme that it is very yll, but I will make a fayrer; and in the meane tyme take heed that none of those that be heere doo see it, for all the world wold know it, for I have made it in haste in theyr presence

I go to my tedious talk. You make me dissemble so much that I am afrayd thereof with horrour, and you make me almost play the part of a traytor. Remember that if it weare not for obeying I had rather be dead. My heart bleedeth for yt. To be short, he will not com but with condition that I shall promise to be with him as heretofore at bed and bord, and that I shall forsake him no more; and upon my word he will doo whatever I will and will com, but he hath prayed me to tarry till after to morrow.

He hath spoken at the fyrst more stoutly, as this bearer shall tell you upon the matter of the Inglishman and of his departure; but in the end he cometh to his gentleness agayn.

He hath told me, among other talk, that he knew well, that my brother hath told me at Stirling that which he had said there, whereof he denyed the half, and

denyis ye ane half, and abone all, yat ever he came in his chalmer. For to mak him traist me, it behovit me to fenzé in sum thingis with him: Thairfoir, quhen he requestit me to promeis unto him, that quhen he was haill we suld have baith ane bed: I said to him fenzeingly, and making me to beleve his promisis, that gif he changeit not purpois betwix yis and that tyme, I wald be content thairwith; bot in the meane tyme I bad him beid that he leit na body wit thairof, becaus, to speik amangis our selfis, the Lordis culd not be offendit nor will evill thairfoir: Bot thay wald feir in respect of the boisting he maid of thame, that gif ever we aggreit togidder, he suld mak thame knaw the lytill compt thay take of him; and that he counsallit me not to purchas sum of thame by him.

Thay for this caus wald be in jelosy, gif at anis, without thair knawledge, I suld brek the play set up in the contrair in thair presence.

He said, verray joyfully, And think zow thay will esteme zow the mair of that? Bot I am verray glaid that ze speik to me of the Lordis; for I beleve at this tyme ze desyre that we suld leif togidder in quyetnes: For gif it wer uthervyse, greiter inconvenience micht come to us baith than we ar war of: bot now I will do quhatever ze will do, and will lufe all that ze lufe; and desyris zow to mak thame lufe in lyke specially that he was in his chamber. But now to make him trust me I must fayne something unto him; and therefore when he desyred me to promise that when he shuld be well we shuld make but one bed I told him fayning to believe his faire promises, that if he did not change his mynd between this tyme and that, I was contented, so as he wold say nothing therof; for (to tell it betwen us two) the lordis wished no yll to him, but did feare lest, consydering the threatening which he made in case we did agree together, he wold make them feel the small accompte they have made of him; and that he wold persuade me to poursue some of them, and for this respecte shuld be in ~~by and by~~ jealousy if at one instance, without their knowledge I did raise the game to the contrary in their presence

And he said unto me very pleasant and merry "Think you that they doo the more esteem you therefore? But I am glad that you talked to me of the lords. I hope that you desyre now that we shall lyve a happy lyfe; for if it weare otherwise, it could not be but greater inconvenience shuld happen to us both than you think. But I will doo now whatsoever you will have me doo. I will love all those that

maner: For, sen thay seik not my lyfe, I lufe thame all equallie. Upon yis point this beirer will schaw zow mony small thingis. Becaus I have over mekle to wryte, and it is lait: I give traist unto him upon zour word. Summa, he will ga upon my word to all places

Alace! I never dissavit ony body: Bot I remit me altogidder to zour will. Send me advertisement quhat I sall do, and quhatsaever thing sall cum thairof, I sall obey zow. Advise to with zourself, gif ze can find out ony mair secreit inventioun by medicine; for he suld tak medicine and the bath at Cragmillar. He may not cum furth of the hous this lang tyme.

Summa, be all that I can leirne, he is in greit suspicioun, and zit notwithstanding, he gevis credit to my word; bot zit not sa far that he will schaw ony thing to me: bot nevertheles, I sall draw it out of him, gif ze will that I avow all unto him. Bot I will never rejoyce to dissaive ony body that traistis in me: Zit notwithstanding ze may command me in all thingis. Have na evill opinioun of me for that caus, be ressoun ze ar the occasion of it zourself; becaus, for my awin particular revenge, I wald not do it to him.

He gevis me sum chekis of yat quhilk I feir, zea, evin in the quick. He sayis this far, yat his faultis wer publeist: bot yair is

you shall love and so you make them to love me also. For so as they seek not my lyfe, I love them all equally." Thereupon I have willed this bearer to tell you many pretty things; for I have too much to write, and it is late, and I trust him upon your word. To be short, he will go anywhere upon my word

Alas! I never deceived any body; but I remitt myself wholly to your will; and send me word what I shall doo, and whatsoever happen to me, I will obey you. Think also yf you will not fynd some invention more secret by phisick, for he is to take physick at Cragmillar and the bathes also, and shall not com fourth of long tyme.

To be short, for that that I can learn he hath great suspicion, and yet, nevertheless trusteth upon my word, but not to tell me as yet anything; howbeit, if you will that I shall avow him, I will know all of him; but I shall never be willing to beguile one that puttith his trust in me. Nevertheless you may doo all, and doo not estyme me the less therefore, for you are the cause thereof. For, for my own revenge I wold not doo it.

He givith me certain charges, and these strong, of that that I fear even to say that his faults be published, but there be that com-

that committis faultis, that belevis thay will never be spokin of; and zit thay will speik of greit and small. As towart the Lady Reres, he said, I pray God that scho may serve zow for your honour: and said, it is thocht, and he belevis it to be trew, that I have not the power of myself into myself, and that because of the refuse I maid of his offeris. Summa, for certanetie he suspectis of the thing ze knaw, and of his lyfe. Bot as to the last, how sone that I spak twa or thré gude wordis unto him, he rejoysis, and is out of dout.

I saw him not this evening for to end your bracelet, to the quhilk I can get na lokkis. It is reddy to thame: and zit I feir that it will bring sum malheur, and may be sene gif ze chance to be hurt. Advertise me gif ze will have it, and gif ze will have mair silver, and quhen I sall returne, and how far I may speik. He inragis when he heiris of Lethingtoun, or of zow, or of my brother. Of your brother he speikis nathing. He speikis of the Erle of Argyle. I am in feir quhen I heir him speik; for he assuris himself yat he hes not an evill opinioun of him. He speikis nathing of thame that is out, nouther gude nor evill, bot fleis that point. His father keipis his chalmer, I have not sene him.

mitt some secret faultis and fear not to have them spoken of lowdely, and that there is speech of great and small. And even touching the Lady Reres, he said "God grant, that she serve to your honour," and that any may not think, nor he neyther, that myne own power was not in myself, seeing I did refuse his offers. To conclude, for a suerety, he mistrustith her of that that you know, and for his lyfe. But in the end, after I had spoken two or three good words to him, he was very merry and glad.

I have not seen him this night for ending your bracelet, but I can fynd no clasps for yt; it is ready thereunto, and yet I fear lest it shuld bring you yll hap, or that shuld be known if you were hurt. Send me word, whether you will have it and more monney, and how farr I may speak. Now so farr as I perceive *I may doo much without you;*[1] guesse you whithir I shall not be suspected. As for the rest, he is mad when he hears of Ledinton, and of you, and my brother. Of your brother he sayeth nothing, but of the Earl of Arguile he doth; I am afraid of him to heare him talk, at the last he assurit himself that he hath no yll opinion of him. He speaketh nothing of these abrode, nither good nor yll, but avoidit speaking of him. His father

---

[1] The French original is added in the margin in Cecil's hand, "J'ay bien la vogue avec vous."

All the Hammiltounis ar heir, that accompanyis me verray honorabilly. All the freindis of the uther convoyis me quhen I gang to sé him. He desyris me to come and sé him ryse the morne betyme. For to mak schort, this beirer will tell zow the rest. And gif I leirne ony thing heir, I will mak zow memoriall at evin. He will tell zow the occasioun of my remaining. Burne this letter, for it is ovir dangerous, and nathing weill said in it: for I am thinkand upon nathing bot fascherie. Gif ze be in Edinburgh at the ressait of it, send me word sone.

Be not offendit, for I gif not ovir greit credite. Now seing to obey zow, my deir lufe, I spair nouther honour, conscience, hasarde, nor greitnes quhat sumevir; tak it, I pray zow, in gude part, and not efter the interpretatioun of zour fals gude-brother, to quhome, I pray zou, gif na credite agains the maist faithful luifer that ever ze had, or ever sall have.

Sé not hir, quhais fenzeit teiris suld not be sa mekle praisit nor estemit, as the trew and faithful travellis quhilk I sustene for to merite hir place. For obtening of the quhilk aganis my natural, I betrayis thame that may impesche me. God forgive me, and God give zow, my only lufe, the hap and prosperitie quhilk your humble and faithful lufe desyris

keepith his chambre; I have not seen him.

All the Hamiltons be here who accompany me very honestly. All the friends of the others doo come allwais, when I go to visitt him. He hath sent to me and prayeth me to see him rise to morrow in the morning early. To be short this bearer shall declare unto you the rest; and if I learne, anything, I will make every night a memoriall thereof. He shall tell you the cause of my stay. Burn this letter, for it is too dangerous, neither is there anything well said in it, for I think upon nothing but upon grief if you be at Edinburgh.

Now if to please you, my deere lyfe, I spare neither honor, conscience, nor hazard, nor greatness, take it in good part, and not according to the interpretation of your false brother-in-law, to whom I pray you, give no credit against the most faythfull lover that ever you had or shall have.

See not also her whose fayned tears you ought not more to regard than the true travails which I endure to deserve her place, for obtayning of which, against my own nature, I doo betray those that could lett me. God forgive me and give you, my only friend, the good luck and prosperitie that your humble and faythfull lover doth wisshe unto

APPENDIX C. 141

unto zow, quha hopis to be schortly ane uther thing to zow, for the reward of my irksum travellis.

It is lait: I desyre never to ceis fra wryting unto zou; zit now, after the kissing of zour handis, I will end my letter. Excuse my evill wryting, and reid it twyse over. Excuse that thing that is scriblit, for I had na paper zesterday quhen I wrait that of ye memoriall. Remember upon zour lufe, and wryte unto hir, and that verray oft. Lufe me as I sall do zow.

Remember zow of the purpose of the Lady Reres.
   Of the Inglismen
   Of his mother
   Of the Erle of Argyle
   Of the Erle of Bothwell
   Of the ludgeing in Edinburgh

you, who hopith shortly to be another thing unto you, for the reward of my paynes.

I have not made one word, and it is very late, although I shuld never be weary in wryting to you, yet will I end, after kissing of your hands. Excuse my evill wryting, and read it over twise. Excuse also that I scribbled, for I had yesternight no paper when took the paper of a memorial. Pray remember your friend, and wryte unto her and often. Love me allwais as I shall love you.[1]

PUBLISHED LATIN VERSION.

Post eaquam ab eo loco discessi ubi reliqueram cor meum, facilis est conjectura qui meus fuerit vultus, cùm planè perinde essem atque corpus sine corde: ea fuit causa cur toto prandii tempore, neque contulerim sermonem cum quoquam, neque quisquam se offerre mihi sit ausus, ut qui judicarent id non esse ex usu.

PUBLISHED FRENCH VERSION.

Estant partie du lieu ou j'avoye laissé mon coeur, il se peut aisément juger quelle estoit ma contenance, veu ce que peut un corps sans coeur ; qui à esté cause que jusques à la disnée je n'ay pas tenu grand propos ; aussi personne ne s'est voulu avancer, jugeant bien qu'il n'y faisoit bon.

---

[1] The directions for the bearer are not given in the English version. The English version is endorsed on the back: "The long lettre written from Glasgow from the Q. of Scotts to the Erle Bothwell." Under this is written in Cecil's hand, "english," with the marks

Ad quatuor passuum millia antequam ad oppidum accessissem, homo honesto loco natus à comite Leviniae ad me venit, atque ejus nomine salutavit: excusavit comitem, quòd non ipse obviàm processisset, id enim quò minùs auderet, in causa fuisse, quòd verbis asperioribus Cunigamium compellâssem. Petivit etiam ut inquirerem de suspicione mea adversus Comitem. Postrema haec sermonis pars, ab ipso, injussa Comitis, erat adjecta.

Ego respondi, nullam adversus timorem esse medicinam; neque si extra culpam esset, tam meticulosum futurum; neque me, nisi ad dubitationes, quae in ejus literis erant, asperiùs respondisse. In summa, imposui homini silentium. Longum esset cetera perscribere. D. Jacobus Hamiltonius mihi obviàm venit; is ostendit superiore tempore, cùm de meo adventu audisset, eum discessisse, ac Hustonum ad se misisse, qui diceret, se nunquam fuisse crediturum, quòd aut ipsum persequeretur, aut Hamiltoniis se conjungeret; se verò respondisse, sui itineris causam unam fuisse, ut me videret, neque cum Stuartis, aut Hamiltoniis, injussu meo, se conjuncturum.

Lussius, Hustonus, Caldoëllii filius, comitati quadraginta circiter equis, obviàm venerunt. Lussus dixit, se a regis patre in eum ipsum diem ut causam diceret

Estant encor à quatre mille pas de la ville, vint à moy un Gentilhomme envoyé par le conte de Lenos, qui me salva en son nom; & l'excusa de ce qu'il ne m'estoit venu au devant, disant, qu'il ne l'avoit osé entreprendre, à cause que j'avoye tensé Cuningham avec paroles aigres. Il me demanda aussi que je m'enquisse de soupçon que j'avoye contre iceluy conte. Ceste derniere partie de son dire avoit esté adjoustée par luy, sans que le Conte luy eust commandé.

Je respondy, qu'il n'y avoit point de remede contre la crainte; & que s'il estoit hors de faute, il ne seroit pas tant timide; & que je n'avoye point respondu asprement sinon aux doutes qui estoient en ses lettres. En somme, j'imposay silence au personnage. Il seroit long descrire tout le reste. Le Seigneur Jaques Hambleton vint au devant de moy, lequel me declara, qu' auparavant ayant entendu ma venüe, il s'estoit retiré, & luy avoit envoyé Huston, pour luy dire, qu'il n'eust jamais creu, ou qu'il l'eust voulu poursuivre, ou qu'il se fut joinct avec les Hambletons; & qu'il respondit, qu'il n'y avoit eu qu'une cause de son voyage, a sçavoir, pour me voir, & qu'il ne se conjoindroit avec les Stuarts & Hambletons sans mon commandement.

Lusse, Huston, & le fils de Cauldwellis, accompagnez d'environ quatre vingts chevaux, vindrent au devant de moy. Lusse dict, que ce jour-là mesme

APPENDIX C. 143

arcersitum, contra quam chirographo promisisset; id chirographum penes se esse; tamen cùm de meo adventu rescitum esset, diem prolatum. Se accersitum a Comite ire nolle, ac jurat se nihil unquam ab eo velle.

Nemo oppidanorum me convenit, quae res facit ut eos credam ab illo stare; praeterea bene loquuntur, saltem de filio. Nullos praeterea nobiles video praeter meos comites.

Rex arcersivit Joachimum heri, ac eum interrogavit, cur non prope se diverterem, id enim si fecissem, se citiùs surrecturum; item cur venissem? an reconciliationis causâ? ac nominatim, an tu hic esses? an familiae catalogum fecissem? an Paridem & Gilbertum accepissem, qui mihi scriberent? an Josephum dimissura essem? Miror quis ei tantum indicarit; etiam, usque ad nuptias Sebastiani sermo pervenit.

Ego cum de suis literis rogavi, in quibus questus erat de quorundam crudelitate; respondit, se non nihil esse attonitum, meumque ei conspectum tam jucundum, ut putaret se laetitiâ moriturum. Offendebatur eo quòd tam cogitabunda essem.

Ego discessi ad coenam. Qui has fert tibi de meo adventu narrabit. Rogavit me ut redirem, quod & feci. Suum mihi morbum explicavit, seque nullum testa-

il estoit adjourné par le pere du Roy, contre ce qu'l avoit promis par son seing & que ce seing estoit par devers luy; mais que quand on fut adverty de ma venüe, que le jour avoit esté prolongé. Et qu'il ne vouloit aller par devers le Conte, qui l'avoit appellé en jurant, qu'il ne luy demanderoit jamais rien.

Nul des citoyens n'est venu à moy, qui faict que je croy qu'ils sont d'avec cestuy-la; & puis ils parlent en bien, au moins du fils. D'avantage je ne voy aucuns de la Noblesse outre ceux de ma suite.

Le Roy appella hier Joachim, & l'interroga, pourquoy je n'alloye loger pres de luy, & que si je le faisoye, il seroit plustost remis fus; item pourquoy j'estoye venue, & si c'estoit pour faire une reconciliation : si vous estiez icy : & si j'avoye faict quelque rolle de mes domestiques : si j'avois prins Paris & Gilbert, afin qu'ils m'escrivissent : & si je ne vouloye pas licentier Joseph. De je m'estonne qui luy en a tant declaré; car mesme ila tenu propos de Sebastien.

Je l'ay enquis de ses lettres, ou il s'estoit plaint de la cruanté d'aucuns. Il respondit, qu'il estoit aucunement estonné, & qu'il se trouvent si joyeux de me voir, qu'il pensoit mourir de joye. Cependant il estoit offensé de ce que j'estois ainsi pensive.

Je m'en allay soupper. Celuy qui vous porte ces lettres vous sera entendre de ma venüe. Il me pria de retourner, ce que je say. Il me declara son mal, adjoustant,

mentum facturum, nisi id unum, quòd omnia mihi relinqueret; me autem sui morbi fuisse, quod molestè tulisset me tam alieno erga se animo fuisse. Ac postea inquit, me rogas quid sibi velit illa crudelitas, cujus mentio est in meis literis? ad te unam id spectat, quae meas pollicitationes ac poenitentium recipere non vis. Fateor à me peccatum esse, sed non in eo quod semper negavi; peccavi etiam adversus quosdam civium tuorum, quod mihi abs te condonatum est.

Ego sum adolescens.
Ac tu dicis, quòd post veniam saepe abs te datam, adhuc ad peccata redeo. Nonne homo, quâ ego sum aetate, consilio destitutus, bis aut ter labi potest, aut pollicitis non stare, ac deinde sui errati poenitere, & rerum usu corrigi? Quòd si veniam impetrare potero, polliceor me nunquam posthac peccaturum. Nihil autem aliud peto, nisi ut communi mensâ & lecto, tanquam conjuges, utamur: ad haec nisi tu consentias, nunquam ex hoc lecto resurgam. Te rogo, ut mihi indices quid decreveris. Novit autem Deus quid paenarum feram, quòd Deum mihi te fecerim, ac nihil aliud nisi te cogitem: quòd si quando te offendo, tu ipsa in causa es, nam cùm aliquis me offendit, si id perfugium haberem, ut apud te queri possem, ad neminem alium querelam deferrem; sed si quid

qu'il ne vouloit point faire de testament, sinon cestuy seul, c'est qu'il me laisseroit tout; & que j'avoye esté la cause de sa maladie, pour l'ennuy qu'il avoit porté que j'eusse l'affection tant esloignée de luy. Et puis apres, Vous me demandez, dit-il, que veut dire ceste cruaute dont je say mention en mes lettres? cela s'addresse seulement à vous, qui ne voulez recevoir mes promesses ny ma repentance. Je confesse que j'ay grandement offensé, mas non en ce que j'ay tousjours desnié; J'ay aussi peché a l'encontre d'aucuns de vos citoyens, ce que vous m'avez pardonné.

Je suis jeune.
Vous dites cependant, qu'apres m'avoir souvent pardonné, je retourne en semblables fautes. Un homme de mesme age que je suis, & destitué de conseil, ne peut il pas faillir deux ou trois fois, ou ne tenir pas quelque fois promesse, & apres se repentir de sa faute, en se corrigeant par l'usage des occurrences? Que si je puis obtenir pardon, je promets cy apres de ne plus offenser. Je ne vous demande rien davantage, sinon que nous ne faisions qu'une table, & un lict, comme ceux qui sont mariez: à cela si vous ne consentez, je ne releveray jamais de ce lict. Je vous prie, de me faire entendre ce que vous avez deliberé: car Dieu sçayt quelle peine je porte, de ce que j'ay fait de vous un Dieu, & que je ne pense à autre chose qu' à vous: que si je vouse offense quelque-

audio, nec te familiariter utor, cogor id in pectore clausum tenere: quae res ita me angit, ut mentem & consilium mihi prorsus excutiat.

Ego semper ei respondebam, sed nimis longum esset omnia perscribere. Rogavi eum cur discessum adornaret in ista nave Anglica. Ille id pernegat, adjecto etiam juramento; sed confessus est se cum Anglis colloquutum. Postea rogavi eum de quaestione Gulielmi Hiegait. Id quoque negavit, donec ipsa verba, quae prolata erant, ei detulissem. Tum dixit se certiorem à Minto factum, dici quendam è concilio literas de se mittendo in carcerem, ac, nisi pareret occidendo, ad me detulisse ut subscriberem: ac se idem ex ipso Minto quaesisse; cumque respondisse, sibi verum videri. De hoc capite cum cras conveniam. Quod ad reliqua de Gulielmo Hiegait, ea confessus est; nec id nisi postridie quàm veneram.

Magnopere cupiebat ut ego in ejus hospitio apud eum diverterem. Ego recusavi, ac dixi ei opus esse purgatione, nec id hic fieri posse. Dixit se accepisse quòd lecticam mecum attulissem; se verò maluisse mecum unà pro-

fois, vous en estes cause, veu que quand on m'offense, si j'avoye ce refuge, que je me peusse plaindre vers vous, je ne feroie ma complainte à autre ; mais si j'entend quelque chose, & que je'naye familiarité avec vous, je suis contraint de la retenir close en mon coeur ; ce qui me tourmente tellement, qu'il m'oste du tout l'entendement & le conseil.

Je luy respondoye tousjours, mais il seroit long de tout escrire. Je luy ay demandé pourquoy il deliberoit s'en aller en ce navire Anglois. Ce qu'il nia, voire avec jurement ; mais il a confessé avoir parlé avec les Anglois. Apres je l'ay enquis touchant la dispute de Guillaume Hiegait. Ce qu'il a aussi desnié, jusques à ce que je luy ay rapporté les mesmes paroles qu'il avoit proferées. Alors il dit, qu'il estoit adverty par Minto, qu'on disoit, qu'un du conseil m'avoit apporté des lettres, afin de les signer, pour le faire mettre en prison, voire s'il n'obeïssoit, pour le tuer. Et qu'il enquist le semblable de Minto, qui respondit, que cela luy sembloit vray. De ce chef je luy en parleray demain. Quant au reste, touchant Guillaume Hiegait, il l'a confessé, mais non jusques au jour d'apres mon arrivée.

Il desiroit fort que J'allasse loger en son hostel ; ce que j'ay refusé, luy disant, qu'il avoit besoin de purgation, & que cela ne se pouvoit faire. Il adjousta, qu'il avoit entendu que j'avoye amené une litiere & qu'il eust

K

ficisci. Credebat, opinor, quòd in carcerem cum aliquò amandatura essem. Ego respondi, quòd ductura mecum essem ad Cragmillarium, ubi & medici & ego possemus ei adesse, neque longè à meo filio abesse. Ille respondit, se, ubi vellem, paratum esse modò de eo quod peteret securum se facerem.

Cupiebat ne à quoquam conspiceretur. Irascitur quoties ei mentionem Walcarii facio, ac se, dicit, aures ei è capite avulsuram, ne mentiri cum ait: nam de hac re eum interrogáram, ac de eo quòd iratus esset quibus dam procerum, atque eis minaretur. Id negat, & ait omnes sibi charos esse, ac me rogat ne quid secus de se crederem. Quod ad me attinet, se malle de vita discedere, quàm quicquam committere quod me offenderet.

Ac postea tantum minutarum adulationum tam moderatè ac tam prudenter mihi effudit, ut tibi res admirationi sit futura. Penè oblita eram, quòd dixit, in hoc negotio Hiegait non posse de me quicquam suspicari; se enim nunquam crediturum, quòd ego, quæ propria ejus caro essem, quicquam mali ei facerem. Etiam se rescisse, quòd ego ei rei subscribere recusâssem: quòd si quis suam vitam peteret, facturum ut satis magno ei constaret: sed sibi neminem nec suspectum esse, nec futurum; sed se omnes dilecturum quos ego diligerem.

mieux aymé aller ensemble avec moy. J'estimee qu'il pensoit que je le voulusse envoyer prisonnier quelque part. Je respondy, que je le meneroye avec moy à Cragmillar, afin que là les medicins & moy le peussions secourir, & que je ne m' esloignasse de mon fils. Il respondit, qu'il estoit prest d'aller, où je voudroye, pourveu que je le rendisse certain de ce qu'il m'avoit requis.

Il desiroit de n'estre veu de personne. Il se fasche toutes les fois que je luy parle de Walcar, & dit, qu'il luy arrachera les oreilles de la teste, & qu'il a menty: car je l'avoye interrogé de cela, & de ce qu'il s'estoit courroucé contre aucuns des seigneurs, & les avoit menassez. Ce qu'il nie, & dit qu'il les ayme tous, & me prie que je ne croye point autrement de luy: & quant à ce qui me touche, qu'il aymeroit mieux mourir, que de faire chose qui me peust offenser.

De apres il m'a usé de tant de petites flateries, avec tel poids & discretion, que vous en seriez estonné. J'avoye, peu s'en faut, oublié ce qu'il dit sur le fait de Hiegait, qu'il ne peut rien soupçonner de moy, & qu'il ne croira jamais que moy, qui suis sa propre chair, luy fasse aucun desplaisir; & qu'il sçavoit bien, que j'avoye refusé de souscrire à cela. Que si quelqu'un cherchoit à luy oster la vie, qu'il seroit en sorte qu'elle luy seroit clerement venduë; mais que nul ne luy estoit, ou seroit suspect; ains qu'il aymeroit tous ceaux que J'aymoye.

Nolebat permittere ut à se discederem, sed cupiebat ut unà secum vigilarem. Ego simulabam omnia videri vera, ac mihi curæ esse, atque excusavi quòd illâ nocte vigilare non possem. Ait se non bene dormire: nunquam vidi eum meliùs habere, aut loqui humiliùs. Ac nisi experimento didicissem, quàm esset ejus cor cereum, meum adamantinum, & quale nullum telum penetrare posset, nisi quod è tua manu veniat, propè erat, ut ejus miserta fuissem: sed ne time, præsidium ad mortem usque custodietur. Tu vide ne tuum capi sinas a gente illa perfida quae non minore contentione tecum de hoc ipso aget.

Arbitror in eadem schola doctos fuisse. Iste semper in oculis habet lacrymam: salutat omnes, etiam usque ad infimos, & miseris modis eos ambit, ut ad sui misericordiam eos perducat. Hodie patri ejus sanguis è naribus & ore fluxit; tu conjice quale id sit præsagium. Nondum eum vidi, continet enim se in cubiculo. Rex poscit ut meis manibus sibi tradam cibum; sed tu nihilo magis istic sis crediturus, quàm ego hîc ero.

Il ne vouloit point permettre que je m'en alasse, mais desiroit que je veilasse avec luy : & je saingnoye que tout cela me sembloit vray, & que je m'en soucioye beaucoup, & en m'excusant, que je ne pouvoye veiller pour ceste nuict-là, il dit, qu'il ne pouvoit bien dormir. Je ne l'ay jamais veu mieux porter, ne parler si doucement ; & si je n'eusse appris par l'experience, combien il avoit le cœur mol comme cire, & le mien estre dur comme diamant, & lequel nul trait ne pouvoit percer, sinon descoché de vostre main, peu s'en eust fallu que je n'eusse en pitié de luy : toutesfois ne craignez point, ceste forteresse sera conservée jusques à la mort ; mais vous regardez que ne laissez surprendre la vostre, par ceste nation infidele, qui avec non moindre opiniastreté debatra le mesme avec vous.

J'estime qu'ils ont esté enseignez en mesme escole. Cestuicy a tousjours la larme à l'oeil ; il saluë tout le monde, voire jusques au plus petits, & les flate d'une façon pitoyable, afin qu'il les ameine jusques à avoir compassion de luy. Aujourd'huy le sang est sorty du nez & de la bouche à son pere ; vous donc devinez maintenant quel est ce presage. Je ne l'ay point encor veu, car il se tient en sa chambre. Le Roy me requiert que je luy donne à manger de mes mains ; or vous n'en croyez pas pardela rien d'avantage, pendant que je suis icy.

Haec est mea primi diei expeditio, eandem cras finiam. Omnia scribo, etsi non sunt magni ponderis, ut tu optima seligendo judicium facias. Ego in negotio mihi maximè ingrato versor. Nunquid subit cupiditas ridendi, videndo me tam bene mentiri, saltem dissimulare tam bene, ac interim vera dicere? Omnia mihi aperuit sub nominibus Episcopi & Sutherlandi; nec tamen adhuc collocuta sum, aut verbo attigi, quicquam eorum quae tu mihi declarâsti; sed tantùm vi adulationum & precum ago, ut à me sit securus: & conquerendo de Episcopo, omnia de eo expiscata sum: cetera audisti.

Nos sumus conjuncti cum duobus infidis hominum generibus: diabolus nos sejungat, ac nos conjungat Deus in perpetuum, ut simus fidissimum par quod unquam junctum est. Haec mea fides est, in ea volo mori.

Excusa quòd malè pingam, dimidium te oportet divinare; sed ego ei rei mederi non possum, non enim optimè valeo; & tamen magnâ fruor laetitiâ scribendo ad te cùm alii dormiunt; quando ego dormire non possum, ut illi faciunt, nec ut ego vellem, hoc est, in tuo complexu, mi care amice, à quo precor Deum ut omnia mala avertat, & quietem mittat. Ego eo ut meam

Voyla ce que j'ay despeché pour mon premier jour, esperant achever demain le reste. Je vous escry toutes choses, encor qu'elles soient de peu d'importance, afin qu'en eslisant les meilleures, vous en fassies jugement. Je suis occupée en une affaire qui m'est infiniement desagreable. Ne vous prent-il pas envie de rire de me voir ainsi bien mentir, au moins de si bien dissimuler en disant verité? Il m'a tout descouvert soubs le nom de l'Evesque & de Sutherland; et toutesfois je ne luy ay encor parlé, ny dit un seul mot, de ce que vous m'avez declaré; ains seulement je le poursuy par force de flateries & prieres, afin qu'il s'asseure de moy. Et me plaignant de l'Evesque, j'ay sçeu toutes choses de luy, & entendu le reste.

Nous sommes conjoints avec deux especes d'hommes infideles; le diable nous vueille separer, & que Dieu nous conjoingne à jamais, à ce que soyons deux personnes tres-fideles, si jamais autres ont esté conjointes ensemble. Voila ma foy, & veux mourir en icelle

Excusez moy que j'escry mal, il faudra que vous en deviniez la moytié: mais je ne puis remedier à cela, car je ne suis pas à mon aise; & neantmoins j'ay une grande joye en vous escrivant pendant que es autres dorment, puis que de ma part je ne puis dormir comme eux, ny ainsi que je voudroye, c'est à dire, entre les bras de mon tres cher amy, du

APPENDIX C.

quetem inveniam in crastinum, ut tum mea biblia finiam ; sed angor quòd ea me à scribendo de me ipsa ad te impediat, quia tam diu est. Fac me certiorem quid, de re quam nosti decreveris, ut alter alterum intelligamus, nequid ob id secus fiat

Ego nudata[1] sum, ac dormitum eo, nec tamen me continere possum, quò minùs quod restat chartae deformiter conscribellem. Malè sit isti variolato, qui me tot laboribus exercet ; nam absque eo esset ut materiam multò elegantiorem ad differendum haberem. Non magnopere deformatus est, multum tamen accepit. Penè me suo enecavit anhelitu ; est enim gravior quàm tui propinqui ; & tamen non accedo propius ad eum, sed in cathedra sedeo ad pedes ejus, cùm ipse in remotissima lecti parti sit

Nuncius patris in itinere

Sermo D. Jacobi Hamiltonii

De eo quod Lussac Comarchus mihi retulit de dilatione.

De quibus interrogavit Joachinum

De ordinatione familiae.

quel, je prie Dieu, qu'il vueille destourner tout mal, & luy donner bon succes : je m'en vay pour trouver mon repos jusques au lendemain, afin que je finisse icy ma Bible ; mais je suis fachée que ce repos m'empesche de vous escrire de mon fait, par ce qu'il dure tant. Faites moy sçavoir ce que vous avez deliberé de faire touchant ce que sçavez, afin que nous nous entendions l'un l'autre, & que rien ne se fasse autrement.

Je suis toute nuë, & m'en vay coucher ; & neantmoins je ne me puis tenir que je ne barbouille encor bien mal, ce qui me reste de papier. Maudit soit se tavelé, qui me donne tant de travaux ; car sans lui j'avoye matiere plus belle pour discourir. Il n'a pas esté beaucoup rendu diforme, toutesfois il en a pris beaucoup. Il m'a quasi tuée de son halene, car elle est plus forte que celle de vostre parent ; & neantmoins je n'approche pas pres de luy ; mais je m'assieds en une chaire à ses pieds, luy estant en la partie du lict plus esloignée

Du messager du pere sur le chemin.

Du dire du sieur Jacques Hambleton.

De ce que le prevost de Lusse m'a rapporté touchant le retardement.

De ce qu'il s'est enquis à Joachim

Du reglement de la famille

---

[1] The Scotch "irkit" was mistaken for naked. The French "Je suis toute nuë" is from the Latin ; but the English "weary" could have been from neither.

De meo comitatu	De ma suite
De causa mei adventûs	De la cause de mon arrivée
De Josepho	De Joseph
Item, De sermone inter me & illum	Item, Du devis d'entre moy & luy
De ejus voluntate placendi mihi, & de ejus poenitentia	De la volonté qu'il a de me complaire, & de sa repentance.
De interpretatione suarum literarum	De l'interpretation de ses lettres
De negotio Gulielmi Hiegait, & de suo discessu	Du fait de Guillaume Hiegait, & de son depart
De domino de Leviston	Du Sieur de Levingstoun

Penè oblita eram, quòd dominus Levistonius D. Reresiae dixit in aurem, dum cœnaret, quòd praebiberet eis quos nôssem, eà lege ut ego rebiberem eorum nomine. Ac post cœnam dixit mihi, dum ad ignem califiebam cùm ei inniterer, Bella, inquit, hujusmodi hominum visitatio; non tamen tanta è tuo accessu potest eis esse laetitia, quanta in molestia quidam hodie relictus est, qui nunquam laetus erit, donec te iterum videbit. Ego de eo quaesivi quisnam is esset. Ille arctiùs corpus meum comprimens, respondit, unus eorum qui te reliquerunt; tu quis sit divinare potes.

Peu s'en faut que je n'aye oublié, comme le Sieur de Levinstoun a dit à l'oreille en soupant à Madamoiselle Reres, qu'elle veut à ceux qu'elle cognoissoit, soubs condition que je le pleigeroye en leur nom. Et apres souper il me dit, comme je me chauffoye aupres du feu estan appuyée sur son espaule, Voyla une belle visitation de telles gens; mais toutesfois la joye de nostre venüe ne leur peut estre si grande, combien est la facherie à celuy qui a esté de laissé seul aujourd'huy, & qui ne sera jamais joyeux, jusques à ce qu'il vous ayt veuë Derechef je luy demanday qui estoit cestuy là; luy m'embrassant plus estroitement me respondit, c'est l'un de ceux qui vous ont laissée. Vous pouvez deviner qui est cestuy-là

Ego hodie elaboravi usque ad horam secundam in hac armilla, ut clavem includerem, quae subtus annexa est duobus funiculis; malè autem facta est ob temporis angustiam, sed faciam pulchriorem. Interim prospice, ne quisquam eorum qui hic sunt videat, quia omnes mortales eam agnos-

J'ay aujourd'huy travaillé jusques à deux heures en ce brasselet, pour y enfermer la clef, qui est jointe au bas avec deux petites cordes. Il est mal fait, à cause du peu de temps qu'on a eu; mais j'en seray un plus beau. Cependant advisez que personne de ceux qui sont icy ne le voye, car tout

cent tantâ festinatione in omnium oculis facta est

Nunc proficiscor ad institutum meum odiosum. Tu me adeo dissimulare cogis, ut etiam ipsa horream; ac tantum non proditricis partes me agere cogis. Illud reminiscere, quòd nisi tibi obsequendi desiderium me cogeret, mallem mori, quàm haec committere; cor enim mihi ad haec sanguinem fundit. Breviter, negat se mecum venturum, nisi eâ lege, ut ei polliccar me communi cum eo mensâ & thoro usuram velut antea, ac ne saepiùs cum derelinquam. Hoc si faciam, quicquid velim faciet, ac me commitabitur; sed me rogavit, ut se expectarem in diem perendinum.

Valde ferociter ab initio loquebatur, uti qui has fert tibi narrabit, de colloquio cum Anglis, de suo discessu; sed tandem reversus est ad suam humanitatem

Inter alia consilia quae mihi retulit, se satis scire, quòd meus frater ad me detulisset, quae ipse cum eo egisset Sterlini; quarum rerum dimidium negavit, ac maximè illud, quòd fratris mei cubiculum esset ingressus. Ut ego faciliùs fidem apud eum assequerer, necesse mihi erat quaedam fingendo ei obsecundare. Quamobrem cùm rogaret ut ei pollicerer, cùm primùm revaluisset; communem nobis fore

le monde le cognoist, tant il a esté fait à la haste devant les yeux de chacun

Maintenant je vien à ma deliberation odieuse. Vous me contraignez de tellement dissimuler, que j'en ay horreur, veu que vous me forcez de ne jouer pas seulement le personnage d'une trahistresse. Qu'il vous souvienne, que si l'affection de vous plaire ne me forçoit, j'aymeroye mieux mourir que de commettre ces choses; car le coeur me seigne en icelles. Bref, il ne veut venir avec moy, sinon soubs ceste condition, que je luy promette d'user en commune d'une seule table & d'un mesme lict, comme auparavant, & que je ne l'abandonne si souvent; Et que si je le fay ainsi. il fera tout ce que je voudray, & me suivra. Mais il m'a prié, que je l'attendisse encor deux jours.

Au commencement il parloit fort asprement, comme vous recitera celuy qui porte les presentes, du devis eu avec les Anglois & de son depart: mais enfin il revint à sa douceur.

Entre autres secrets qu'il me recita, il dit, qu'il sçavoit bien, que mon frere m'avoit rapporté ce qu'il avoit fait avec luy à Stirling, des quelles choses il a nié la moytié, & principalement, qu'il fust entré en la chambre de mon frere. Et afin qu'il me creust plustost, j'estoye contrainte de luy accorder quelque chose en dissimulant: parquoy lors qu'il me priast que je luy promisse, qu'incontinent qu'il seroit guery,

lectum, ego dissimulanter dixi, ac fingens me bellis ejus pollicitationibus fidem habere, me consentire, nisi ille interea propositum mutaret; sed interea videret ne quisquam id resciscerct, propterea quòd proceres nostris colloquiis offendi non possent, nec ideo malè velle : sed in timore futuros quod comitatus fuisset, si aliquando inter nos concordes essemus, se daturam operam ut intelligerent quàm parvi eum aestimássent; item, quòd mihi consuluisset ne gratiam quorundam seorsum à se expeterem. Has ob causas eos in magna suspicione futuros, si ego faciem scenae ad contrariam huic fabulam instructae, in presentia, eis insciis turbarem.

Tum ille vehementer lætus subjecit, Et tu putas ne quod pluris illi te aestimabunt ob hunc causam? Sed valde gaudeo quòd sermonem de proceribus injecisti ; nunc quidem credo te cupere, ut unà concorditer vivamus : nam ni ita esset, majora quàm uterque timemus incommoda utrique possent evenire ; sed nunc, quod tu vis, volo, & quod amabis amabo ; & cupio ut eorum similiter concilies amorem : quia postquam non petunt vitam meam, omnes amo ex aequo. Circa hoc caput hic tabellarius multa minuta tibi declarabit : quia nimis multa supersunt scribenda, & jam serum est. Huic adhibebis fidem juxta tuum verbum. Breviter, meo jussu quovis ibit.

nous ne faisions plus qu'un lict, je luy dy par dissimulation, en saingnant, que je croyoye à ses belles promesses, que je l'y accorderoye, pourveu qu'il ne changeast d'advis ; mais cependant, qu'il regardast que personne n'en sçeust rien, parce que les Seigneurs ne pourroient estre offensez de nos propos, ny consequemment nous en vouloir mal. Ains seroient en crainte de ce qu'il m'auroit suivy. Et si nous pouvions estre d'acord ensemble, qu'il pourroit donner ordre, qu'ils entendroient combien peu ils l'avoient estimé. Item, de ce qu'il m'avoit conseillé, que je troubloye ainsi maintenant la face du theatre, qui avoit esté appresté pour jouër une autre fable.

Alors estant grandement joyeux il adjousta, et pensez-vous que pour cela ils vous en estiment d'avantage ? Mais je suis bien aise que vous avez fait mention des Seigneurs ; maintenant je croye, que vous desirez que nous vivions ensemblement en paix ; car s'il estoit ainsi, beaucoup plus grandes fascheries nous pourroient advenir à tous deux, que nous ne craignons ; mais à present je veux ce que vous voulez & aimeray ce que vous aimerez ; & desire que pareillement vous acquiriez leur amitié : car puis qu'ils ne pourchassent à m'oster la vie, je les aime tous esgalement. Touchant ce chef, le porteur vous recitera plusieurs particularitez ; d'autant qu'il y a trop de choses qui restent à escrire, & qu'il est desia tard :

Hei mihi! nunquam quemquam decepi; sed ego me in universum tuae voluntati subjicio. Fac me certiorem quid faciam, & quicunque sequatur eventus, tibi obsequor. Etiam tecum perpende, comminisci queas aliquam occultiorem rationem per medicinam; sumpturus est enim & medicinam, & balneum ad Cragmillarium. Non potest domo egredi ad multos dies.

Breviter, quantum intelligere possum, in magna suspicione versatur, nihilo tamen minùs magnam habet fidem orationi meae; nec tamen usque adeo ut quicquam mihi effutiat: nihilo minùs ego ex eo, siquidem tu vis, omnia apud eum profitear & agnoscam. Sed nunquam gaudebo in quovis homine qui mihi fidit, decipiendo; nihilo minùs tu mihi potes omnibus in rebus imperare. Noli ideo sinistram opinionem de me concipere; quia tu ipse hujus vi mihi author es; nunquam enim istud in eum committerem, meae propriae ultionis causâ.

Interim me attingit in loco suspecto; idque ad vivum hactenus proloquutus est, sua crimina esse palam; sed sunt qui majora committant, & opinantur ea silentio tegi; & tamen homines de magnis juxtà & parvis loquuntur. D. Reresia ait, Deum precor, ut officia quae tibi praestat, sint tibi honori: ait etiam quosdam

Vous adjousterez foy selon vostre parole. En somme, il ira ou vous voudrez par mon commandement.

Helas! je n'ay jamais trompé personne; mais je me submets en toutes choses à vostre volonté. Faictes moy sçavoir ce que je doy faire; & quoy qu'il en puisse advenir, je vous obeiray. Et pensez en vous mesme, si pouvez trouver quelque moyen plus couvert que par breuvage; car il doit prendre medicine, & estre baigné à Cragmillar. Il ne peut sortir du logis d'icy à plusieurs jours.

Brief, à ce que j'en puis entendre, il est en grand soupçon; neantmoins il adjouste beaucoup de foy à ma parole; mais non encores tant, qu'il n'en descouvre quelque chose; toutesfois je confesseray, & recongnoistray tout devant luy, si vous le trouvez bon. Mais si ne m'esiouiray-je jamais à tromper celuy qui se sie en moy: neantmoins vous me pouvez commander en toutes choses. Ne concevez donc point de moy aucune sinistre opinion, puis que vous-mesmes estes cause de cela; car je ne le feroye jamais contre luy pour ma vengeance particuliere.

Cependant il m'a donné attainte du lieu suspect, & a jusques icy discouru bien au vif, que ces fautes son congneuës; mais qu'il y en a qui en commettent de plus grandes, encores qu'ils estiment qu'elles soient cachées par silence; & toutesfois que les hommes parlent des grands aussi bien que des petits. Quant à Reres, il dit, je

credere, ac se id verum existimare, me non habere potestatem mei intra me, idque quia recusaverim conditiones à se oblatas. Breviter, certum est quòd de eo quod scis, suspicetur, ac de vita etiam. Quòd ad posterius, cùm primùm ego duobus aut tribus bonis verbis eum compello, gaudet, ac timere desinit.

Non vidi eum hac vesperâ, quia tuam armillam conficiebam, cui nullam possum ceram invenire, id enim unum ad perfectionem ei deest; & adhuc vereor ne aliquod se offerat infortunium, & conspici possit, si te contingat laedi. Fac me certiorem num eam velis habere, & si plusculum pecuniae velis habere, & quando debeam redire, & quem in loquendo modum mihi statuam. Insanit ad mentionem de Lethintonio, de te, de fratre meo. De tuo fratre nihil loquitur. De Comite Argatheliae in timore versor, quoties cum audio loquentem; jus certo habet eum nihil de se malè opinari. De eis qui extrà sunt nihil, neque boni neque mali, loquitur, sed semper hunc locum vitat. Pater ejus domi se continet, nondum enim vidi.

Omnes Hamiltoni hic adsunt, & me comitantur valde honorificè. Alterius omnes amici me comi-

prie Dieu que les services qu'elle vous fait, vous soient à honneur. Il dit aussi, qu'il y en a qui croient, & que de sa part il l'estime veritable, que je n'ay point en moy el puissance de moy-mesme, d'autant que j'ay refusé les conditions qu'il avoit offertes. Brief, il est certain qu'il se doute de ce que scavez, & de sa vie mesmes. Quant au reste, soudain que je luy propose deux ou trois bonnes paroles, il se resiouit, & n'a point de crainte.

Je ne l'ay point veu ceste apresdisnée, parce que je faisoye vostre brasselet, auquel je ne puis accommoder de la cire; car c'est ce qui defaut à sa perfection; & encor je crain, qu'il n'y survienne quelque inconvenient, & qu'il soit recogneu, s'il advenoit que vous fussiez blessé. Faictes moy entendre si vous le voulez avoir, & si avez affaire de quelque peu plus d'argent; & quand je doy retourner, & quel ordre je tiendray à parler à luy. Il enrage quand je fay mention de Lethington, de vous & de mon frere. Il ne parle point de vostre frere. Quant au Conte d'Argathley, je suis en crainte, toutes les fois qu'il en devise. Il s'asseure qu'il ne pense point de mal de luy. Quant à ceux qui sont de dehors, il n'en parle ny en bien, ny en mal, seulement il a evité tousjours ce lieu. Son pere se tient tousjours au logis, & ne l'ay point encores veu. Tous les Hambletons sont icy, qui me sont compagnie assez honnorable. Tous les amis de

tantur quoties cum viso. Petit à me ut cras tempori adsim, ut eum surgentem videam. Ut paucis absolvam, hic tabellarius reliqua tibi narrabit. Si quid novi hic discum, vesperi faciam commentarium. Ille tibi explicabit meae morae causam. Crema has literas, sunt enim periculosae, nec quicquam bene in eis dictum ; ego enim nihil cogito nisi molestias. Si fueris Edinburgi cùm has accipies, fac me certiorem.

Noli offendi, quia non nimium fido. Nunc postquam ob studium tibi obsesequendi, me chare amice, neque honori, neque conscientiae, nec periculis, neque quant aevis magnitudini parco ; rogo in bonam partem accipias, ac non juxta interpretationem fallacis fratris uxoris tuae, cui rogo nullam adhibeas fidem adversus fidelissimam omnium quas aut habuisti, aut habebis, amicam.

Noli eam intueri, cujus fictae lachrymae non debent tanti esse, quanti fidi labores, quos ego perfero, ut merear in ejus locum succedere ; quem ut obtineam ego eos prodo, idque adversus ingenium meum, qui impedimento esse possent. Deus mihi det veniam, & Deus tibi det, mi unice amice, cum successum, & felicitatem, quam tua humilis & fidelis amica tibi optat, quae brevi sperat aliud de te in praemium mei molesti laboris.

l'autre me suivent lorsque je le visite. Il me prie, qui je soye demain assez à temps pour le voir lever. Afin que je le face court, ce porteur vous dira le surplus. Si j'appren icy quelque chose le soir, je le mettray en memoire. Il vous declarera la cause de mon retardement. Bruslez ces lettres, car elles sont dangereuses, & s'il n'y a rien que soit bien couché ; je ne pense que choses fascheuses. Si vous estes à Edinbourg, quand vous recevrez ces lettres, faictes-le moy sçavoir.

Ne vous offensez point, si je me fie par trop. Maintenant donc, mon cher amy, puis que pour vous complaire, je n'espargne, ny mon honneur, ny ma conscience, ny les dangers, ny mesmes ma grandeur quelle qu'elle puisse estre ; je vous prie, que vous le preniez en la bonne part, & non selon l'interpretation du faux frere de vostre femme, auquel je vous prie aussi n'adjouster aucune foy contre la plus fidele amye que vous avez euë, ou que vous aurez jamais.

Ne regardez point à celle, de laquelle les feinctes larmes ne vous doivent estre de si grand poix, que les fideles travaux que je souffre, afin que je puisse meriter de parvenir en son lieu. Pour lequel obtenir, je trahi, voire contre mon naturel, ceux qui m'y pourroient empescher. Dieu me le vueille pardonner, & vous doint, mon amy unique, tel succez & felicité, que vostre humble & fidele amye le souhaitte, laquelle espere en brief autre recompense

Serum est: tamen nunquam cupio cessare à scribendo ad te; tamen nunc post oscula manuum tuarum, finem meis literis imponam. Excusa meam in pincendo imperitiam, easque relege. Excusa cursionem characterum, quia heri chartam non habebam, cùm id quod in commentario erat, scriberem. Reminiscere tuae amicae, ac saepe ad eam rescribe. Redama me uti ego te amabo.

  Reminiscere sermonis de Rerisia.
  De Anglis
  De matre ejus
  De comite Argatheliae
  De comite Bothueliae
  De hospitio Edinburgi

de vous, pour ce mien facheux labour.

Il est tard, neantmoins je ne desire jamais cesser de vous escrire; et toutesfois, apres vous avoir baisé les mains, je seray fin à mes lettres. Excusez mon ignorance à escrire, & relisez mes lettres. Excusez la briefueté des characteres, car hier je n'avoye point de papier, quand j'escrivi ce qui est au memoire. Ayez souvenance de vostre amye, & luy rescrivez souvent. Aimez moy, comme je vous aime: & Ayez memoire du propos de Madamoiselle Reres.

  Des Anglois.
  De sa mere.
  De conte d'Arghley.
  Du conte de Bothwel.
  Du logis d'Edimbourg.

Letter III.

[This letter was not published in the Latin edition of Buchanan's *Detection*, nor in the Rochelle French translation. The only versions extant are the original French and the Scots.]

Original French Version.

(In the Record Office State Papers, Mary Queen of Scots, vol. ii. No. 66.)

Monsieur si lenuy de vostre absence celuy de vostre oubli la crainte du dangier, tant promis d'un chacun a vostre tant ayme personne peuvent me consoller Je vous en lesse a juger veu le malheur que mon cruel sort et continuel malheur mavoient promis a la suite des infortunes et craintes

Scots Version.

(Published in the Scots version of Buchanan's *Detection*.)

My Lord, gif the displesure of zour absence, of zour forzetfulness, ye feir of danger sa promisit be everie ane to zour sa luifit persone, may gif me consalatioun, I leif it to zow to juge, seing the unhap that my cruell lot and continuall misadventure hes hitherto promysit me, following ye misfor-

APPENDIX C.

tant recentes que passes de plus longue main les quelles vous scaves mais pour tout cela Je me vous accuserai ni de peu de souverance ni de peu de soigne et moins encore de vostre promesse violee que ce qu'il vous plaist mest agreable et sont mes penses tant volontereinent, aux vostres asubjectes que je veulx presupposer que tout ce que vient de vous procede non par aucune des causes susdictes anis pour telles qui son justes et raisoinables et telles que Je desir moy mesme qui est lordre que maves promis de prendre final pour la scincte et honnorable service du seul soubtein de ma vie pour qui seul Je la veus conserver et sens lequel Je ne desire que breve mort or est[1] pour vous tesmoigner combien humblement sous voz commandemens Je me soubmets Je vous ay envoie en signe d'homage par paris lornement du cheif conducteur des aultres membres inferant que vous investant de sa despoille de luy qui est principae le rest ne peult que vous estre subject et avec ques le consentement du cueur au lieu du quel puis que le vous ay Ja lesse Je vous envoie un sepulcre de pierre dure poinct de noir semc d'larmes et de ossement, la pierre Je le la compare a mon cueur qui comme luy est taille en un seur tombeau ou receptacle de voz commandements et sur tout de vostre nom et memoire qui y sont enclos, comme mes chevculz eu la bagne pour Jamais neu sor-

tunes, and feiris as weill of lait, as of ane lang tyme bypast, the quhilk ze do knaw. Bot for all that, I will in na wise accuse zow, nouther of zour lytill remembrance, nouther of zour lytill cair, and leist of all of zour promeis brokin, or of ye cauldnes of zour wryting, sen I am ellis sa far maid zouris, yat yat quhilk pleisis zow is acceptabill to me; and my thochtis ar sa willingly subdewit unto zouris, that I suppois yat all that cummis of zow proceidis not be ony of the causis foirsaid, but rather for sic as be just and ressonabill, and sic as 1 desyre myself. Quhilk is the fynal order that ze promysit to tak for the suretie and honorabil service of ye only uphald of my lyfe. For quhilk alone I will preserve the same, and without the quhilk I desyre not but suddane deith. And to testifie unto zow how lawly I submit me under zour commdementis, I have send zow, in signe of homage, be Paris, the ornament of the heid, quhilk is the chief gude of the uther memberis, inferring thairby that, be ye seising of zow in the possesioun of the spoile of that quhilk is principall, the remnant cannot be bot subject unto zow, and with consenting of the hart. In place quhairof, sen I have ellis left it unto zow, I send unto zow ane sepulture of hard stane, colourit with blak, sawin with teiris and bones. The stane I compare to my hart, that as it is carvit in ane

[1] "Est" for "et."

tir que la mort ne vous permet fair trophee des mes os comme la bagne en est remplie en signe que vous aves fayt entiere conqueste de moy, de mon cueur et jusque a vous en lesser les os pour memoir de v̄re victoire et de mon agreable perte et volontiere pour estre mieux employe que Je ne les merite Les maie demiron[1] est noir qui signifie la fermete de celle que lenvoie les larmes sont sans nombre ausi sont les craintes de vous desplair les pleurs de vostre absence et de desplaisir de ne pouvoir de ne pouvoir estre en effect exterieur vostre comme je suys sans faintise de cueur et desprit et a bon droit quant mes merites seroint trop plus grands que de la plus perfaite que Jamais peut et telle que je desire estre et mettray poine en condition de contre fair pour dignement estre emploit soubs vostre domination resents[2] la donc mon seul bien en aussi bonne part, comme avecques extreme Joie Jay fait vostre mariage, qui jusques a celuy de nos corps en public ne sortira de mon sein, comme merque de tout ce que Jay ou espere ni desire de felicite en ce monde or craignant mon cueuer de vous ennuyer autant a lire que je me plaire descrir Je finiray apres vous avoir baise les mains daussi grande affection que je prie Dieu (O le seul soubtien de ma vie) vous la donner longue et heureuse et a moy v̄re bonne grace le seul bien que je desire et sure sepulture or harbour of zour commandementis, and abone all, of zour name and memorie that ar thairin inclosit, as is my hear in this ring, never to cum forth, quhill deith grant unto yow to ane trophee of victorie of my banes, as the ring is fullit, in signe that yow haif maid ane full conqueis of me, of myne hart, and unto yat banes my banes be left unto yow in remembrance of your victorie and my acceptabill lufe and willing, for to be better bestowit then I merite. The ameling that is about is blak, quhilk signifyis the steidfastnes of hir that sendis the same. The teiris ar without number, sa ar the dreddouris to displeis yow, the teiris of your absence, the disdane that I cannot be in outwart effect youris, as I am without fenzeitnes of hart and spreit, and of gude ressoun, thocht my meritis wer mekle greiter then of the maist profite that ever was, and sic as I desyre to be, and sall tak pane in conditiounis to imitate, for to be bestowit worthylie under your regiment. My only wealth, ressaif thairfoir in als gude part ye same, as I have ressavit your marriage with extreme joy, the qubilk sall not part furth of my bosum, quhill yat mariage of our bodyis be maid in publict, as signe of all that I outher hope or desyris of blis in yis warld. Zit my hart feiring to displeis you as mekle in the reiding heirof, as I delite me

---

[1] "Demiron" for "d'environ."
[2] "Resents" for "reseves" ("receves").

a quoy je tends Jay dit a ce porteur ce que Jay apris sur luquel Je me remets sachant, le credit que luy donnes comme fait celle qui vous veult estre pour Jamais humblee et obeisante loyalle femme et seulle amye qui pour Jamais vous voir[1] entierement le cueur le corps sans aucun changement comme a celuy que J posseur[2] fait possesseur du cueur du quel vous pouves tenir seur Jusques a la mort ne changera car mal ni bien onque ne estrangera.

———

[Indorsed on the back in Cecil's hand " ② frenche lre." And in the hand of a clerk, "To prouf the affectioun."]

in ye writing, I will mak end, efter that I have kissit zour handis with als greit affectioun as, I pray God (O) ye only uphald of my lyfe) to gif yow lang and blissit lyfe, and to me zour gude favour, as the only gude yat I desyre, and to ye quhilk I pretend. I have schawin unto this beirer that quhilk I have leirnit, to quhome I remit me, knawand the credite that ze gaif him, as scho dois that will be for ever unto zow humbill and obedient lauchfull wyfe, that for ever dedicates unto zow hir hart, hir body, without ony change, as unto him that I have made possessour of hart, of quhilk se may hald zow assurit, yat unto ye deith sall na wayis be changeit, for evill nor gude sall never mak me go from it.

LETTER IV.

ORIGINAL FRENCH VERSION AT HATFIELD.

(See Calendar of Hatfield Manuscripts, vol. i. pp. 376–77.)

J'AY veille plus tard la hault que je n'eusse fait si ce neust esté pour tirer ce que ce porteur vous dira que Je treuve la plus belle

PUBLISHED FRENCH VERSION OF 1573, TRANSLATED FROM THE LATIN.

J'AYE veillé plus tard la haut, que jen'eusse fait, si ce n'eust esté pour tirer ce que ce porteur vous dira ; que je trouve la plus belle

---

PUBLISHED LATIN VERSION.

Diutius illic morata sum quàm volebam, nisi id factum fuisset ut aliquid ex eo exsculperem, quod hic tabellarius tibi indicabit ; quae est bellissima occasio quae se poterat offere ad excusandum nostra negotia. Promisi me ipsum cras ad eum aducturam. Tu rem cura, si tibi commoda videtur.

Nunc, domine, ego pactum violavi ; quia tu veluisti ne vel

---

[1] " Voir " for " voue."   [2] " Posseur " written above in another hand.

commoditie pour excuser vostre affaire que se pourroit presenter. Je luy ay promise de le luy mener demain si[1] vous le trouves bon mettes y ordre. Or mon sieur j'ay ja rompu ma promesse Car vous ne mavies comande[1] vous envoier ni escrire si ne le fais pour vous offencer et si vous scavies la craint que j'en ay vous nauries tant des subçons contrairs que toutesfois je cheris comme procedant de la chose du mond que je desire et cherche le plus bonne c'est votre[1] grace de laquelle mes deportemens m'asseureront et je n'en disesperay Jamais tant que selon vostre promesse vous m'en dischargeres vostre coeur aultrement je penseras que mon malheur et le bien composer de ceux qui n'ont la troisiesme partie de la fidelité ni voluntair obéissance que je vous porte auront gaigné sur moy l'avantage de la seconde amye de Jason. Non que je vous compare a un si malheureuse ni

commodité pour excuser vostre affaire, qui se pourroit presenter. J'ay promis, que je luy meneray demain cestuy-là. Vous aiez en soin, si la chose vous semble commode.

Maintenant j'ay violé l'accord ; car vous aviez deffendu que je n'escrivisse, ou que je n'envoyasse par devers vous ; neantmoins je ne l'ay faict pour vous offenser. Et si vous sçaviez en quell crainte je suis à present, vous n'auriez point tant de soupçons contraires en vostre esprit; lesquels toutesfois je supporte, & pren en bonne part, comme provenans de la chose que je desire le plus de toutes celles qui sont soubs le ciel, & que je poursuy avec extreme diligence, à scavoir vostre amitié, dont tant de devoirs que je say me rendent certaine, & assurée. Quant à moy, je n'en desespereray jamais, & vous prie, qui suivant vos promesses, vous me faciez entendre vostre affection : autrement j'estimeray que cela se faict par mon malheureux destin, & par la

scriberem, vel mittarem ad te. Non tamen hoc feci quo te offenderem. Et si scires quanto in metu ego sum in praesentia, non tot in animo haberes contrarias suspiciones ; quibus tamen ego faveo & boni consulo, tanquam profectis ab ea re, quam ego omnium quae sub coelo sunt maximè cupio & diligentissimè persequor, qui est tuus favor ; de quo mea me officia certàm & securam facient. Quod ad me attinet, nunquam de eo desperabo ; ac te rogo, ut juxta tua promissa animum tuum mihi exponeres ; alioqui suspicabor fieri malo meo fato, & fiderum favore erga illas, (quae nec tertiam habent partem fidelitatis, & voluntatis tibi obsequendi, quam ego habeo) ut ipsae, velut secunda Jasonis amica, me invitâ, priorem apud te locum gratiae occupaverint ; nec

---

[1] "De" is added in the margin by another hand.

APPENDIX C.

moy a une si impitoiable. Combien que vous men fassies un peu resentir en chose qui vous touschat ou[1] pour vous preserrer et garder a celle a qui seulle vous aporteins si lon se peult approprier ce que lon acquiert par bien et loyalment voire uniquement aymer comme je fais et fairay toute ma vie pour pein ou mal que m'en puisse avenir. En recompence de quoy et des tous les maulx dont vous maves este cause, souvenes vous du lieu icy pres. Je ne demande que vous me tennes promesse de main mais que nous truvions[2] et que nadjoustics foy au subçons quaures sans nous en certifier, et Je ne demande a Dieu si non que coignoissies tout ce que je ay au coeur qui est vostre et quil vous presence de tout mal au moyns durant ma vié qui ne me sera chere qu' autant qu'elle et moy vous serons agreables. Je m'en vois coucher et vous donner le bon soir mandes moy demain faveur des astres envers celles, qui toutesfois n'ont une tierce partie de loyauté, & volonté que j'ay de vous obeïr, si elles, comme si j'estoye une seconde amye de Jason, malgré moy, occupent le premier lieu de faveur; ce que je ne dy pour vous accomparer à cet homme en l'infelicité qu'il avoit, ny moy avec une femme toute esloignée de misericorde, comme estoit celle-là. Combien que vous me contraignez estre en aucune partie semblable à elle, en toutes les choses qui vous concernent, ou qui vous peuvent garder, & conserver à celle, à laquelle seule vous estes entierement de droict: car je vous puis m'attribuer comme mien, qui vous ay aquis seul loyaument, en vous aimant aussi uniquement comme je fay, & feray tant que je vivray, me rendant assurée contre les travaux & dangers qui en pourront advenir. Et pour tous ces maux, desquels m'avez esté la cause, rendez moy ceste faveur, que vous ayez sou-

---

hoc eo dico, quo te cum homine, eâ quâ ille erat infelicitate, comparem, nec me cum muliere tam aliena à misericordia quàm illa erat: quanquam tu me cogis aliqua ex parte ut illi sim similis omnibus in rebus quae ad te pertinent, aut quae te servare & custodire queant illi, cujus unius jure totus es; siquiden id tanquan meum mihi vindicare possum, quod paravi te unum fideliter, imo unicè amando (quod & facio, & faciam dum vixero) secura omnis laboris & periculi, quae illinc impendere poterunt. Et ob haec omnia mala, quorum tu mihi causa fuisti, hanc repende gratiam, ut loci memineris qui hic vicinus est.

Non postulo ut cras mihi promissa serves, sed ut congrediamur, & ut nullam fidem suspicionibus adhibeas, nisi rebus exploratis. Ego

---

[1] " Ou," correction by another hand instead of some illegible word.
[2] The " n " in " trouvions " corrected from " m " by another haud.

comme vous seres porté a bon heur. Car j'enseray en pein et faites bon guet si l'oseau sortira de sa cagé ou sens son per[1] comme la tourtre demeurera seulle a se pour lamenter de l'absence ˄ court quelle sort-le que Je ne puis faire ma lettre de bon coeur si ce nestoit que je ay peur que soyes endormy. Car je nay ose escrire devant Joseph et bastienne et Joachim qui ne sont que partir quand J'ay commence.

[Endorsed by Cecil " (3) french Ire," and in a clerk's hand " Lettre concerning Halyruid house."]

venance de lieu qui est prochain d'icy.

J ne demande pas que vous me temez promesse demain ; ains que nous assemblions, & que n'adjoustiez point de foy aux suspicions, sinon apres l'experience faicte. Je ne demande autre chose à Dieu, fors qu'entendiez ce que j'ay en l'esprit, qui est vostre ; & qu'il vous garentisse de tout mal, au moins pendant que je seray en vie, laquelle je ne tien point chere, sinon, en tant que moy & elle, vous sommes agreables. Je m'en vay coucher, & vous dy à Dieu. Faites moy certaine de bon matin de vostre portement ; car je seray en peine jusques à ce que je l'entende. Comme l'oyseau eschappé de la cage, ou la tourtre, qui est sans compagne, ainsi je demeureray seule, pour pleurer vostre absence, quelque brieve qu'elle puisse estre. Cest lettre sera volontiers ce que je ne pourray faire moy-mesmes, si d'aventure comme je crain vous ne dormez defia. Je n'ay osé escrire en pre-

verò nihil aliud à Deo peto, nisi ut ea intelligas quae sunt in animo meo, qui est tuus : & ut te praeservet ab omni malo, saltem dum mihi supererit vita quam & ego non duco mihi caram nisi quatenus & ego, & illa tibi placemus. Ego eo cubitum, & tibi vale dico. Fac me certiorem summo mane de tua valetudine ; ego enim ero in molestia donec intelligam. Si avis evaserit è cavea, aut sine compare, velut turtur, ego remanebo sola ut lamenter absentiam tuam quamlibet brevem. Haec epistola libenter faciet quod ego ipsa facere non potero, nisi forte tu, quod metuo, jam dormias. Non sum ausa scribere praesentibus Josepho, Sebastiano & Joachimo, qui nihil aliud quàm discesserant, cùm ego coepi haec scribere.

---

[1] " Per" originally " pere," the final " e " struck out by another hand.

APPENDIX C.

sence de Joseph, Sebastian, &
Joachim, qui ne faisoient que de
partir quand j'ay commencé à
escrire ces choses.

PRINTED SCOTS TRANSLATION.

I have walkit laiter thair up
then I wald have done, gif it
had not bene to draw sum-
thing out of him, quhilk this
beirer will schaw zow; quhilk is
the fairest commoditie that can be
offerit to excuse zour affairis. I
have promysit to bring him to
him the morne. Put ordour to
it, gif ze find it gude.

Now, Schir, I have brokin my
promeis: because ze commandit
me nouther to wryte nor send
unto zow. Zit I have not done
this to offend zow. And gif ze
knew the feir yat I have presently,
ze wald not have sa mony contrary suspiciounis in zour thocht;
quhilk notwithstanding I treit and
chereis, as proceeding from the
thing in the world I maist desyre,
and seikis fastest to haif, quhilk
is zour gude grace; of the quhilk
my behaviour sall assure me. As
to me, I sall never dispair of it,
and prayis zow, according to zour
promeis, to discharge zour hart
unto me. Utherwayis I will
think that my malhure, and the
gude handling of hir that hes not
ye third part of the faithfull nor
willing obedience unto zow that I
beir, hes wyn, aganis my will, yat
advantage over me, quhilk the
second lufe of Jason wan; not
that I will compair zow unto ane

ENGLISH TRANSLATION AT HATFIELD.

I have watched later then there
above than I wold haue don, if it
had not bene to draw out that
that this bearer shall tell you,
that I fynde the fayrest commoditie to excuse yor busynes that
might be offred: I have promised
him to ҏ bring him to morrowe.
Yf you think, it give ordre thereunto. Now S^r I have not yet
broken my promes w^t you for
   not
you had ˄ commanded me
nothing And to send you any
thing or to write and I doo it not,
for offending of you. And if you
knew the feare that I am in
therof, you wold not have so
many contrary suspiciōs, w^{ch}
nev^{r}theless I cherishe as proceeding
from the thing of this worlde that
I desyre and seeke the moste,
that is yor favo^r, or good will, of
wch my behaviour shall assure me,
And I will nev^r dispayre thereof
           yor
as long as according to my promes
youw shall discharge yor harte to
me, Otherwise I wold think
that my yll luck, and the fayre
behavio^r of those that have not
the thirde parte of the faythful-
nes and voluntary obedience that
I beare unto you, shall have
wonne the advantage ov^r me the
advantage of the second Loover of

sa unhappy as he was, nor zit myself to ane sa unpietifull ane woman as scho. Howbeit ze caus me to be sumthing lyke unto hir in ony thing that tuichis zow, or yat may preserve and keip zow unto hir, to quhome only ze appertene; gif it be sa that I may appropriate that quhilk is wyn throch faithfull, zea, only luifing of zow, as I do, and sall do all the dayis of my lyfe, for pane or evill that can cum thairof. In recompense of the quhilk, and of all the evillis quhilk ze have bene caus of to me, remember zow upon the place heir besyde.

I craif with that ze keip promeis to me the morne; but that we may meit togidder, and that ze gif na faith to suspiciounis without the certanetie of thame. And I craif na uther thing at God but that ze may know that thing that is in my hart quhilk is zouris; and that he may preserve zow from all evill, at the leist sa lang, as I have lyfe, quhilk I repute not precious unto me, except in sa far as it and I baith ar aggreabill unto zow. I am going to bed, and will bid zow gude nicht. Advertise me tymely in the morning how ze have fairin; for I will be in pane until I get worde. Mak gude watch, gif the burd eschaip out of the caige, or without hir mate. As ye turtur I sall remane alone for to lament the absence, how schort yat sa ever it be. This letter will do with ane gude hart, that thing quhilk I cannot

Jason. Not that I doo compare you to so wicked a ~~person~~, or myself to so unpitifull a person, Althoughe you make me feele some greefe in a matter that toucheth you, and to preserve & keepe you to her whō alone you belong, if a body may clayme to him selfe that wch is wōn by ———[1] well, faythfully, yea enticrly loving, as I doo, & will doo all my lyfe for payne or hurt what soev^r may happen to me thereby. In recompence whereof, and of all the evils that you bene cause of to me, Remember the place ~~nighe~~ hereby. I desyre not that you keepe promes w^t me to morrowe, but that we may be togither, and that you give no credit to the suspicions that you shall have, w^tout being assured thereof. And I aske no more of God but that you might know all that I have in my harte, wch is yours and that he preserve you frō all evill, at the leist during my lyfe, wch shall not be deere unto me, but as long as y^t & I shall please you. I go to bed, and give you good night. Send me word tomorrow early in the morning how you have don for I shall thing long. And watche well if the byrde shall fly out of his cage or w^tout his ~~father~~ make as the turtle shall remayne alone to lament & morne for absence how short soev^r it be. That that I could not doo my lfē shuld doo it w^t a good will, yf it weare not that I feare to wake you, for I

[1] Illegible word struck out.

| do myself gif it be not that I have feir that ze ar in sleiping. I durst not write this befoir Joseph, Bastiane, and Joachim, that did bot depart evin quhen I began to wryte. | durst not write before Joseph & Bastian & Joachim, who weare but new gon from I begon.

[Endorsed "Copy, 3, english."

Endorsed in another hand, "(3) lre concerning Holly Roode House."] |
|---|---|

Letter V.

Original French Version.	Published French Version Translated from the Latin.
(In the Record Office State Papers, Mary Queen of Scots, vol. ii. No. 63.)	
Mon coeur helas! fault il que la follie d'une famme dont vous connoisses asses l'ingratitude vers moy soit cause de vous donner displesir veu que je neusse sceu y remedier sans de le scavoir; et despuis que men suit apersue je ne vous lay peu dire pour scavoir comment je me gouvernerois car en cela ni autre chose je ne veux entreprandre de rien fayre sans en scavoir votre voloutay, laquelle je vous suplie me fayre	Mon coeur helas faut-il que la folie d'une femme dont vous cognoissez assez l'ingratitude vers moy, soit cause de vous donner deplaisir, veu que je n'y pouvoye mettre remede, sans les donner à cognoistre? Et depuis que je m'en suis apperceuë, je ne le vous pouvoye dire, pource que je ne sçavoye pas comme m'y gouverner. D'autant qu'en cecy, ny en autre chose, je ne veux point entreprendre de rien faire, sans que je

Scots Translation.

My hart alace! must the follow of ane woman quhais unthankfulness toward me ze do sufficiently knaw be occasion of displesure unto zow, considering yat I culd not have remidit thairunto without knawing it? And sen that I persavit it, I culd not tell it zow, for that I knew not how to governe myself thairin; For nouther in that, nor in any uther thing, will I tak upon me to do ony thing without knawledge of zour will, quhilk I beseik zow let me understand; for I will follow it all my lyfe, mair willingly than zow sall declair it to me; and gif ze do not send me word this nicht quhat ze will that I sall do, I will red myself of it, and hazard to caus it to be interprysit

entandre car je la suivray toute ma vie plus volontiers que vous ne me la declareres, et si vous ne me mondes ce soir ce que volles que jeu faisse je m en deferay au hazard de la fayre entreprandre ce qui pourroit, nuire a ce a quoy nous tandons tous deux, et quant elle sera marice je vous suplie donnes qune opinion sur aultrui ne nuise en votre endroit a ma constance. Soupsonnes moi may quant je vous en veulx rendre hors de doubte et mesclersir ne le refuses ma chere vie et permettes que je vous face preuve par mon obeissance de ma fidelité et constance et subjection volontaire, que je prends pour la plus agreable bien que je scaurois rescevoir si vous le voulles accepter, et nen faytes la ceremonie car vous ne me scauriez davantage outrasger ou donner mortel ennuy

[Endorsed in Cecil's hand :— "④ french lettre ;" and in the

cognoisse quelle est vostre volonté, que je vous supplie me faire entendre ; car je l'executeray toute ma vie, voire plus volontiers que ne me le voudriez declarez : que si vous ne me mandez des nouvelles ceste nuit, de ce que vous voulez que je face, je m'en depescheray, & me hazarderay de l'entreprendre, ce que pourroit nuire à ce que nous desseignons tous deux. Et quand elle sera mariée, je vous prie de m'en donner une autre, ou bien j'en prendray quelqu'une, dont j'estime que la façon vous contentera ; mais quant à leur langue & fidelité envers vous, je n'en voudroye pas respondre. Je vous supplie, que l'opinion d'une autre n'esloingne vostre affection de ma constance. Vous meffiez vous de moy, qui vous veux mettre hors de doute, & declarer mon innocence, & ma chere vie, ne le refusez pas, & ne souffrez que je vous donne espreuve de mon obeissance fidelité constance, & voluntaire subjection, que je prend à tres grand plaisir, autant que je le

---

and takin in hand, quhilk micht be hurtfull to that quhairunto baith we do tend. And quhen scho sall be maryit I beseik zow give me ane, or ellis I will tak sic as sall content zow for their conditiounis ; bot as for thair toungis or faithfulness towart yow I will not answer. I beseik zow yat ane opinioun of uther persoun be not hurtfull in your mynde to my constancie. Mistrust me ; but quhen I will put zow out of dout, and cleir myselfe, refuse it not, my deir lufe, and suffer me to mak zow sum prufe be my obedience, my faithfulness constancie, and voluntarie subjectioun, quhilk I tak for the plesandest gude that I micht ressaif, gif ze will accept it ; and mak na ceremonie at it, for ze culd do me na greiter outrage, nor give mair mortall greif.

hand of a clerk "anent the despeche of Margaret Carwood—q[lk] was before hir marriage—pruifs her affection."]

puis avoir, si vous l'acceptez sans ceremonie car vous ne me, sçauriez faire plus grand outrage, ny offence plus mortelle.

Letter VI.

Original French Version at Hatfield.

Monsieur, helas pourquoy est vostre fiance mise en personne si indigne, pour subçonner ce que est entierement vostre.[1] Vous m'avis promise que resouldries tout et me[2] que ˄ manderis tous les jours ce que j'aurais a faire. Vous nen aves rien fait. Je vous advertise bien de vous garder de vostre faul<u>x beau frere</u>[3] Il est venu vers <u>moy et sens me monstrer rien</u> de vous me dist que ~~vous~~ luy mandies qu'il vous escrive ce qu'auries a dire, et ou, et quant vous me troveres et ce que faires touchant luy et la dessubs m'a preschè que c'estoit une folle entrepri~~n~~se, et qu' avecques mon honneur Je ne vous pourries Jamaiis espouser, veu qu'estant marié vous m'amenies et que ses gens ne l'enduroient pas et que les seigneurs se dediroient. Somme il est tout contrair. Je luy ay dist qu'estant venue si avant si vous ne vous en retiries de vous mesmes que persuasion ne la mort mesmes ne me fairoient faillir ~~de~~ ᵃ ma promesse. Quant au lieu vous estes trop neli-

Published French Translation.

Monsieur, helas pourquoy est vostre fiance mise en personne si indigne pour soupçonner ce qui est entierement vostre? j'enrage vous m'aviez promis, que vous vous resouldriez en toutes choses, & que chacun jour vous m'envoiriez dire ce que j'auroye à faire. Vous n'en aviez rien fait. Je vous veux bien advertir que vous preniez bien garde à vostre desloyal beau frere : il vint vers moy, sans me faire apparoistre que c'estoit de vostre part, & me dit, que vous l'aviez requis, qu'il vous escrivit ce que je vous voudroye dire, & où, & quand je pourroye aller à vous, & ce que vous deliberiez faire de luy ; & sur cela il me remonstra, que c'estoit une folle entreprise, & que pour mon honneur je ne vous pourvoye prendre à mary, puis que vous estiez marié, ny aller avec vous, & que ses gens mesmes ne le souffriroient pas, voire que les Seigneurs contrediroyent à ce que en seroit proposé. Bref, il semble qu'il nous soit du tout contraire. Je luy respondy, veu que y'en estoye venuë si avant, que si vous

---

[1] "J'enrasge" inserted in margin. [2] "Me" inserted by another hand.
[3] "E. of Huntly" written on the margin in another hand.

gent (pardonnes moy) de vous en remettre a moy. Choisisses le vous mesmes et me le mandes. Et cependant je suis malade je differeray Quant au propose cest trop tard. Il n'a pas tius a moy que n'ayes pense a heure. Et si vous neussies non plus changé de ~~propos~~ ^pensee depuis mon absence que moy vous ne series a demander telle resolution. ^Or il ne manque rien de ma part et puis que vostre negligence vous met tous deux au danger d'un faux frere, s'il ne succede bien je ne me releveray Jamais. Il vous envoy ce porteur. Car Je ne m'ose me fier a vostre frere de ces lettres ni de la diligence, il vous dira en quelle estat Je suis, et Juges quelle amendemente m'a porté ce incertains Nouvelles. Je voudrois estre morte. Car Je vois tout aller mal. Vous prometties bien autre chose de vostre providence. Mais l'absence peult sur vous, qui aves deux cordes a vostre arc. Depesches la responce a fin que Je ne faille et ne ^vous fies de ceste entreprinse a vostre frere. Car il la dist, et si y est tout contrair

Dieu vous doint le bon soir.

[Endorsed by Cecil "(5) frech;" and in the hand of a clerk, "from Sterling affore the Rawissement.—Pruifis hir mask of Rawissing."] A facsimile of this copy—which

ne vous retractiez, nulle persuasion, non pas mesmes la mort, me seroit manquer à ma promesse. Touchant la place, pardonnez-moy, si je vous dy que vous estes trop negligent de vous remettre à moy. Choisissez-la donc vous-mesmes & m'en advertissez : cependant je ne suis à mon aise, car il est ja trop tard, & n'a pas tenu à moy que vous n'y ayez pensé de bonne heure. Et si vous n'eussiez changé d'opinion depuis mon absence, non plus que moy, vous ne demanderiez maintenant d'en estre resolu. Tant y a qu'il n'y a point de faute de ma part ; & en cas que vostre negligence ne nous mette tous deux au danger d'un desloyal beau frere, si les choses ne succedent, jamais ne puisse-je bouger de ceste place. Je vous envoye ce porteur, d'autant que je n'ose commettre ces lettres à vostre beau frere qui n'usera aussi de diligence. Il vous dira de mon estat. Jugez quel amendement m'ont apporté ces nouvelles ceremonies. Je voudroye estre morte, car je voy que tout va mal. Vous me promistes bien autre chose par vos premieres promesses ; mais l'absence a pouvoir sur vous, qui avez deux cordes en vostre arc. Depechez vous de me faire response, afin que je ne faille ne me voulant fier en vostre frere, car il en a babillé, & y est du tout contraire. Dieu vous donne la bonne nuict.

is written in a "Roman" hand—is printed by Baron de Lettenhove in the *Bulletin de l'Académie Royale de Belgique*, 2 ser. v. 34.

PUBLISHED SCOTS TRANSLATION.

Allace! my Lord, quhy is zour traist put in ane persoun sa unworthie, to mistraist that quhilk is haillely zouris? I am wod. Ze had promysit me, that ze wald resolve all, and yat ze wald send me word every day quhat I suld do. Ze haif done nathing yairof. I advertisit zow weill to tak heid of zour fals brother in law; He come to me, and without schawing me ony thing from zow, tald me that ze had willit him to wryte to zow that that I suld say, and quhair and quhen ze suld cum to me, and that that ze suld do tuiching him; and thairupon hes preichtt unto me yat it was ane fuliche interpryse, and that with myne honour I culd never marry zow, seing that being maryit ze did cary me away, and yat his folkis wald not suffer it, and that the Lordis wald unsay yameselfis, and wald deny that they had said. To be schort, he is all contrarie. I tald him, that seing, I was cum sa far, gif ze did not withdraw zour self of zour self, that na perswasioun, nor deith itself suld mak me fail of my promeis. As tuiching the place ze are to negligent, pardoun me, to remit zour self thair of unto me. Cheis it zour self, and send me word of it; And in the meane tyme I am seik,

ENGLISH TRANSLATION AT HATFIELD.

Alas my Lorde, why is yor trust putt in a pson so unworthy to mistrust that wch is wholly yours! I am wood. You had promised me that you wold resolve all, And that you wold send me worde every daye what I shuld do. You have don nothing thereof. I advertised you well to take heed of yor falce brother in lawe. He cam to me and w'out shewing me any thing from you told me that you had willed him to write to you that that I shuld saye, and where and whan you should com to me, and that that you shuld doo touching him. And therupon hath preached unto me that it was a foolish enterprise and that w^t myn hono^r I could nev^r marry you seing that being maryed you did carry me away. And that his folk wold not suffer yt. And that the Lords wold unsaye themselves and wold deny that they had said. To be shorte he is all contrary. I told him that seing I was com so farre, if you did not w^{t}drawe yo^{r}selfe of yo^{r}selfe that no psuasion nor death it selfe shuld make me fayle of my promesse. As touching the place you are to negligent (pdon me) to

I will differ, as tuiching the mater it is tó lait. It was not lang of me yat ze have not thocht thairupon in time. And gif ze had not mair changeit zour mynd, sen myne absence, then I have, ze suld not be now to ask sic resolving. Weill, thair wantis nathing of my part; and seing that zour negligence dois put us baith in the danger of ane fals brother, gif it succedet not weill, I will never ryse agane. I send this beirer unto zow, for I dar not traist zour brother with thir letteris, nor with the diligence. He sall tell zow in quhat stait I am, and judge ze quhat amendment yir new ceremonies have brocht unto me. I wald I wer deid, for I só all gais ill. Ze promysit uther maner of mater of zour foirseing, bot absence hes power over zow, quha haif twa stringis to zour bow. Dispatch the answer that I faill not, and put na traist in zour brother for this interpryse, for he hes tald it, and is also all aganis it. God give zow gude nicht.

remitt yo^rself thereof unto me. Choose it yo^rselfe and send me word of it. And in the mean tyme I am sicke. I will differ as touching the matter it is to late. It was not long of me that you have not thought thereupon in tyme. And if you had not more changed yor mynde since myne absence than I have, you shuld not be now to ask such resolving. Well ther wantith nothing of my pte. And seeing that yor negligence doth putt us both in ye danger of a false brother, if it succeede not well, I will nev^r rise agayne. I send this bearer unto you for I dare not trust yor broth^r w^t these lres nor w^t the diligence. He shall tell you in what state I am, and judge you what amendement these new ceremonies have brought unto me. I wold I weare dead. For I see all goith yll. You promised other manner of matter of your forseing, but absence hath powre ov^r you, ~~hath~~ who have ij strings to yor bowe. Dispatche the annsweare that I fail you not. And put no trust in yor broth^r for this enterprise. For he hath told yt, and is all against it. God give you good night

[Endorsed " Copie from Sterafore [1]

ling ~~after~~ the ravissm^t. Prufs her mask of Ravishing "]

---

[1] Correction "afore" in Cecil's hand.

Letter VII.

Published Scots Translation.	Published French Translation.
Of the place and ye tyme I remit my self to zour brother and to zow. I will follow him, and will faill in nathing of my part. He findis mony difficulties. I think he dois advertise zow thairof, and quhat he desyris for the handling of himself. As for the handling of myself, I hard it ains weill devysit. Methinkis that zour services, and the lang amitie, having ye gude will of ye Lordis, do weill deserve ane pardoun, gif abone the dewtie of ane subject yow advance yourself, not to constrane me, bot to assure yourself of sic place neir unto me, that uther admonitiounis or forane perswasiounis may not let me from consenting to that that ye hope your service sall mak yow ane day to attene. And to be schort, to mak yourself sure of the Lordis, and fré to mary; and that ye are constraint for your suretie, and to be abill to serve me faithfully, to use ane humbil requiest joynit to ane importune actioun. And to be schort, excuse yourself, and perswade thame the maist ye can, yat ye ar con-	Du lieu, & de l'homme je m'en rapporte à vostre frere & à vous. Je le suivray, & ne faudray en rien de ma part. Il trouve beaucoup de difficultez; je pense qu'il vous en a adverty, & de ce qu'il desiroit, pour bien jouer son personnage. Quant à jouer le mien, je seay comme je m'y dois gouverner souvenant de la façon que les choses ont esté deliberées. Il me semble que vostre long service, & la grande amitié & faveur que vous portent les seigneurs, meritent bien que vous obteniez pardon, encor qu'en cecy vous vous avanciez aucunement par dessus le devoir d'un subjet. Or est-il que vous entreprenez de le faire, non pas afin de me forcer, & tenir captive, ains pour vous rendre assuré pres de moy, & que les remonstrances & persuasions des autres ne m'empeschent de consentir à ce que vous esperez que vostre service vous sera un jour obtenir. Bref, c'est pour vous asseurer des seigneurs, & vous mettre en liberté de vous marier; comme y estant constraint pour vostre seureté, à ce que puis apres me servant loyaument, vous me puissez presenter une humble requeste, conjointe toutesfois avec importunité. Excusez vous donc, & les persuadez le plus que pourrez, que vous estes forcé par necessité de

straint to mak persute aganis zour enemies. Ze sall say eneuch, gif the mater or ground do lyke yow; and mony faire wordis to Lethingtoun. Gif ye lyke not the deid, send me word, and leif not the blame of all unto me.

faire ainsi vostre poursuite à l'encontre de vos ennemis. Vous aurez dequoy dire assez, si l'argument, & le subjet vous plaist; & donnez beaucoup de belles paroles à Ledington. Que si cela ne vous semble bon, advertissez m'en, & n'en mettez pas du toute la faute fur moy.

LETTER VIII.

SCOTS VERSION.

My Lord, sen my letter writtin, zour brother in law yat was, come to me verray sad, and hes askit me my counsel, quhat he suld do efter to morne, becaus thair be mony folkis heir, and amang utheris the Erle of Sudderland, quha wold rather die, considdering the gude thay have sa laitlie ressavit of me, than suffer me to be caryit away, thay conducting me; and that he feirit thair suld sum troubil happin of it: Of the uther syde, that it suld be said that he wer unthankfull to have betrayit me. I tald him, that he suld have resolvit with zow upon all that, and that he suld avoyde, gif he culd, thay that wer maist mistraistit.

He hes resolvit to wryte to zow be my opinioun; for he hes abaschit me to sé him sa unresolvit at the ueid. I assure myself he will play the part of an honest man: But I have thocht gude to advertise zow of the feir he hes yat he suld be chargeit and accusit of tressoun to ye end yat,

PUBLISHED FRENCH TRANSLATION.

Monsieur, depuis ma lettre escrite, vostre beau frere, qui fust, est venu à moy fort triste, & m'a demandé mon conseil de ce qu'il feroit apres demain, pource qu'il y a beaucoup de gens icy, & entre autres le Conte de Southerland, qui aymeroient mieux mourir, veu le bien que je leurs ay fait depuis n'a gueres, que de souffrir que je fusse emmenée, eux me conduisans; & d'autre part qu'il craint, que s'il en survenoit quelque trouble, on ne l'estimast ingrat, comme s'il m'avoit trahie. Je luy dy, qu'il devoit estre resolu de cela avec vous, & mettre hors de sa maison ceux desquels on se meffioit le plus.

Souvant ce mien advis, il s'est resolu de vous en escrire; & me suis estonnée de le voir si peu resolu en temps de necessité. Je m'assure bien qu'il sera toute d'honneste homme; mais je vous ay bien volu advertir de la crainte qu'il a d'estre chargé & accusé de trahison, à ce que, sans

without mistraisting him, ze may be the mair circumspect, and that ze may have ye mair power. For we had zisterday mair than iii. c. hors of his and of Levingstounis. For the honour of God, be accompanyit rather with mair then les; for that is the principal of my cair.

I go to write my dispatche, and pray God to send us ane happy enterview schortly. I wryte in haist, to the end ye may be advysit in tyme.

vous meffier de luy vous y regardiez de plus pres, & que vous vous rendiez d'autant plus fort. Car nous avions hier plus de trois cens chevaux des siens, & de Leviston. Pour l'amour de Dieu soyez plustost accompagné de trop, que de trop peu; car c'est le principal de mon soucy.

Je m'en vay achever ma depeche, & prie Dieu, que nous nous puissions entrevoir bientost en joye. Je vous escry en diligence afin que soyez adverty a temps.

LETTER IX.
THE FRENCH "SONNETS."

O DIEUX ayez de moy compassion,
Et m'enseignez quelle preuve certain
Je puis donner qui ne luy semble vain
De mon amour & ferme affection.
Las! n'est il pas ja en possession
Du corps, du coeur qui ne refuse pain
Ny dishonneur, en la vie incertain,
Offense de parents, ne pire affliction?
Pour luy tous mes amcs j'estime moins que rien,
Et de mes ennemis je veux esperer bien.

J'ay hazardé pour luy & nom & conscience:
Je veux pour luy au monde renoncer:
Je veux mourir pour luy auanscr.

En reste il plus pour prouver ma constance?
Entre ses mains & en son plein pouvoir
Je metz mon filz, mon honneur, & may vie,
Mon pais, mes subjectz mon ame assubjectie
Est tout à luy, & n'ay autre vaulloir
Pour mon object que sans le decevoir
Suiure je veux malgré toute l'envoie
Qu'issir en peult, car je n'autre è vie
Que de ma foy, luy faire appercevoir
Que pour tempeste ou bonnace qui face
Jamais ne veux changer demeure ou place.
Brief je feray de ma foy telle preuve,

Qu'il cognoistra sans fainte ma constance,
Non par mes pleurs ou fainte obeyssance
Comme autres ont fait, mais par divers espreuve.

Elle pour son honneur vous doibt obeyssance
Moy vous obeyssant j'en puis recevoir blasme
N'estat, à mo regret, comme elle vostre femme
Et si n'aura pourtant en ce point pre-eminence
Pour son profit elle use de constance,
Car ce n'est peu d'honneur d'estre de voz biens dame
Et moy pour vous aimer j'en puis recevoir blasme
Et ne luy veux beder en toute l'observance
Elle de vostre mal n'à l'apprehension
Moy je n'ay nul repos tant je crains l'apparence
Par l'aduis des parentz, elle eut vostre accointance
Moy maugré tous les miens vous porte affection
Et de sa loyauté prenez ferme asseurance.

Par vous mon coeur & par vostre alliance
Elle à remis sa maison en honneur
Elle à jouy par vous la grandeur
Dont tous les siens n'ayent nul asseurance
De vous mon bien elle à eu la constance
Et à gaigne pour un temps vostre coeur
Par vous elle à eu plaisir en bon heur,
Et pour vous à receu honneur & reverence,
Et n' à perdu fin on la jovissance
D'un fascheux sot qu'elle aymoit cherement.
Je ne la playns d'aymer donc ardamment,
Celuy qui n' à en sens, ny en vaillance,
En beauté, en bonté, ny en constance
Point de seconde. Je vis en ceste foy.

Quant vous l'amiez, elle usoit de froideur.
Sy vous souffriez, pour s'amour passion
Qui vient d'aymer de trop d'affection,
Son doig monstroit, la tristesse de coeur
N'ayant plaisir de vostre grand ardeur
En ses habitz, mon estroit sans fiction
Qu'elle n'avoit paour qu'imperfection
Peust l'effacer hors de ce loyal coeur.
De vostre mort je ne vis la peaun
Que meritoit tel mary & seigneur.
Comme de vous elle à eu tout son bien
Et n' à prisé ne jamais estimé
Un si grand heur si non puis qu'il n'est sien
Et maintenant dit l'avoir tant aymé.

Et maintenant elle commence à voir
Qu'elle estoit bien de mauvais jugement
De n'estimer l'amour d'un tel amant
Et voudroit bien mon amy decevoir,
Par les escriptz tout fardez de scavoir
Qui pourtant n'est en son esprit croissant
Ains emprunté de quelque autheur luisant,
A faint tres bien un envoy sans l'avoir
Et toutes fois ses parolles fardez,
Ses pleurs, ses plaincts remplis de fictions.
Et ses hauts cris & lamentations
Ont tant gaigné qui par vous sont gardez.
Ses lettres escriptes ausquelles vous donnez foy
Et si l'aymez & croyez plus que moy.

Vous lay croyez las! trop je l'appercoy
Et vous doutez, de ma ferme constance,
O mon seul bien & mon seul esperance,
Et ne vous puis je asseurer de ma foy
Vous m'estimez leger que je voy,
Et si n'avez en moy nul asseurance,
Et soupconnez mon coeur sans apparence,
Vous deffiant à trop grand tort de moy.
Vous ignorez l'amour que je vous porte
Vous soupconnez qu'autre amour me transporte,
Vous estimez mes parolles du vent,
Vous depeignez de cire mon las coeur
Vous me pensez femme sans jugement,
Et tout sela augmente mon ardeur.

Mon amour croist & plus en plus croistra
Tant que je viuray, and tiendray à grandeur,
Tant seulement d'avoir part en ce coeur
Vers qui en fin mon amour persistra
Si tres à clair que jamais n'en doutra,
Pour luy je veux rechercher les grandeur,
Et feray tant qu'en vray cognoistra,
Que je n'ay bien, heur, ne contentement,
Qu' à l'obeyr & servir loyaument.
Pour luy jattend toute bonne fortune.
Pour luy tout vertu de suiure j'ayenvie
Et sans changer me trouvera tout une.

Pour luy aussi je jette maintes larmes.
Premier quand il se fist de ce corps possesseur,
Du quel alors il n'avoit pas le coeur.
Puis me donna un autre dur alarme
Quand il versae de son sang mainte dragme

Dont de grief il me vint laisser
doleur,
Qui m'en pensa oster la vie, &
frayeur
De perdre las ! le seul rempar qui
m'arme,
Pour luy depuis jay mesprise
l'honneur.
Ce qui nous peult seul pourvoir de
bonheur.
Pour luy depuis jay hazardé
grandeur & conscience.
Pour luy tous mes parentz j'ay
quite, & amis,
Et tous autres respectz sont apart
mis,
Brief de vous seul je cherche
l'alliance.

De vous je dis seul soustein de
ma vie
Tant seulement je cerche m'asseurer,
Et si ose de moy tant presumer
De vous gaigner maugre toute
l'envie.
Car c'est le seul desir de vostre
chere amie,
De vous servir & loyaument
aymer,
Et tous malheurs moins qui rien
estimer,
Et vostre volonte de la mien ne
sujure,
Vous cognostrez avecques obeyssance
De mon loyal devoir n'omittant
lascience
A quoy je estudieray pour tous-
iours vous complaire
Sans aymer rien que vous, soubz
la subjection

De qui je veux sans nulle fiction
Vivre & mourir & à ce j'obtem-
pere.
Mon coeur, mon sang, mon ame, &
mon soucy
Las, vous m'avez promis qu'aurons
ce plaisir
De deviser avecques vous à loysir,
Toute la nuict, ou je languis icy
Ayant le coeur d'extreme paour
transy
Pour voir absent le but de mon
desir
Crainte d'oublier un coup me
vient a saisir :
Et l'autre fois je crains que
rendurcie
Soit contre moy voystre amiable
coeur
Par quelque dit d'un meschant
ramporteur
Un autre fois je crains quelque
aventure
Qui par chemin detou ne mon
amant,
Par un fascheux & nouveau
accident
Dieu detourne toute malheureux
augure

Ne vous voyant selon qu'avez
promis
J'ay mis la main au papier our
escrire
D'un different que je voulu trans-
crire,
Je ne scay pas quel sera vostre
advis
Mais je scay bien qui mieux aymer
scaura
Vous diriez bien que plus y
gaignera.

APPENDIX D.

I.

ACT OF SECRET COUNSEL.

Apud Edinburgh, quarto die mensis Decembris, Anno Dom. 1567.

THE whiche daie my Lorde Regentis Grace, the Lordes of Secrete Counsale and uthers, Baronis, and men of jugement above written, being convenit in counsale, it was proponit unto them that the parliament now approchis, wheirin the cause of the apprehension and reteninge of the Quene our Soverane Lord's moder, mon be debaitit, ressonit and tryit, and it found and declarit, quhither the Noblemen and others quhilkis tuke armes before the saied apprehension, and whiche joyned with them and assistit them at that time or ony wise sensyne, has donne the dewtie of Noblemen, gud subjectis, and nawise offendit nor transgressit the lawes in that fact, or anie thing depending thairon, outher preceding or followinge the same, or not: and in caise it be found that they have not offendit, but done their dewtie, how and be what meane a full and perfect law and securitie maie be obtanit and maid for all them, that other be deid, counsale, or subscription hes enterit in that cause sen the beginninge. The matter being largelie and with gud deliberacion ressonit at great length, and upon sundry daies, at last all the saied Lords, Baronis, and others above expremit, can find no other way or moyen how to find or make the saied securitie, but be oppynynage and reveling of the trewth and grund of the haill matter fra the beginninge plainlie and uprichtlie, quhilk (in sa far as the manifestation theirof maie tend to the dishonor or disestimation of the Quene) they air maist loith to entre in, for that luif they beare unto hir person, wha somtime was theire Soveraine, and for the reverrence of his Majestie, whais moder she is, as alsua thay mony gude and excellent gifts and virtues quharewith God sometimes indowit hir, gif otherwise the sinceritie of their intentions and procedings from the beginninge mycht be known to forrein nacions, and the inhabitantes of this ile (of whome mony yit remains in suspence in jugement) satisfiet and resolvit of the richtnesness of theire quarrel, and the securitie of them, and theire posteritie be ony other meane myght be providit and established. But sen God will suffer no wickitnes to be hid, and that all actions otherwise foundat nor on the simple and nakit trewth, what apperance that evir they have, has na continewance nor stabilitie: Theirfore the Lords of Secrete Counsale, Baronis and men of jugement above expremit, desires it to be found and declarit be the Estates and haill body of the Parliament, that the cause and occasion of the previe conventionis and messages of the Erles, Lords, Noblemen and Baronis, and others faithful and trew subjects, and consequentlie theire taking of armes and cominge to the fields with oppin and

displait baneris, and the cause and occasion of the taking
of the Quene's person upon the 15th daie of Junii last
bypast, and holding and deteininge of the same within
the hous and place of Lochlevin continewallic sensyne,
presentlie, and in all tymes comyng; and generallie all
other things inventit, spokin, writtin, or donne be them,
or aney of them, sen the tent daie of February last bypast
(upon quhilk daie umquhile King Henric, the Quene's
lawfull husband, and our Soveraine Lord the King's
dearest father was shamefully and horriblie murtherit)
unto the daie and date heirof, toweching the saied Quene
hir person, that caus, and all things depending theiron,
or that anie wise maie apperteine theirto, the intromissioun
with the disponinge upon hir propertie, casualties, or
other thing whatsoever perteining, or myght pertene to
hir, was in the saied Quene's awin default, in as far as
be divers hir previe lettres writtin and subscrivit with
her awen hand, and sent by hir to James Erll Boithwell,
cheiffe executor of the said horrible murdor, aswell before
the committing theirof, as therafter, and be hir ungodlie
and dishonorable proceding in a priveit marriage with him
soddanlie and unprovisitlie yarefter, it is most certeine
that she was previe, art and part, and of the actual devise
and deid of the foirmencionit murther of the Kinge, hir
lawchfull husband, our Sovereine Lorde's father, committit be the said James Erll Boithuill, his complices and
partakers; and theirfore justlie deservis whatsoever hes
bin attemtit or shall be usit toward hir for the said caus:
Which murther although be mony indirect and colorat
meanes she and the saied Erll zaid about to collour and to
hold bak the knowledge of the trewith theirof; yit all
men in their harts wer fully perswaided of the authors

and devisers of that mischevous and unworthie fact, awaiting quhill God suld move the harts of som to enter in the quarrell of revenging of the same. And in the meaine time a great part of the Nobilitie, upon just feire to be handillit and demanit in scamblable manner, as the King had bene of befoire, persaivinge the Quene so thrall and bludy affeccionat to the privat appetite of that tyran, and that she and he had conspired togidder sic horrible cruelties, being theirwith garnysit with a companie of ungodllie and vicious persons redy to accomplishe all theire unlawehfull commaundments, of whome he had a sufficient nomber continewallie awaiting upon him for the same effect: All noble and vertuous men abhoring theire traine and companie, but chiefly suspecting, that they, who had sa tressonablie put doune and distroit the father, suld make the innocent Prince, his only sonne, and the principall and almost onlie compfort sent be God to this afflictit nacion, to tast of the same coupe, as the mony inventit purposes to pas where he wes, and where the Noblemen in that opin confusion prevelie reposit them selfs, gave sufficient warning and declaraccion. Quheirfore the seid Erlls, Lordes, Barronis and utheris, faiethfull and trewe subjects, taking armes, or otherwise whatsumever joyning and assisting in the said action, in the said convencionis, taking armes, displaying of banners, coming to the feilds, taking and reteining of the Quene's person, aswell in times bypast, as heirefter, and all other things movid or done be them, or anie of them, touching that caus, and all things depending theiron, or that oniewise maie apperteine theirto, the intromission with or disponinge upon hir propertie, casualties, or other thingis whatsomever perteining or myght perteine to hir, wes alluterlie in default of hir selfe and the saied Erll Boithuill, and be the horrible murther and crueltie of our Soverein Lord's father, conspirit, devisit, committit and concelit be them, colorit and not condignlie punist be them, and theire perfitt counsale. And that the saied Erlls, Lordes, Barronis, and others faithfull and trewe subjects convenit at ony convencions efter the saied murther, for farthering of the triall theirof, and als they and all others that weire on the filds, tuke armes, tuke, held, kepit, and detenit, presentlie holds, keipis, and detens hir person, or sall heirafter, or that hes joynit and assistit them in that quarrell sensyne, and towching the haill premisses, ar, wer, and sall be innocent, fré, and quit of the same, and of all action and cause, criminall or civile, that maie be intentit or persewit agains them or anie of them theirfore, in time cominge. And that a parte of the Thré Estats forsaieds, Prellats, Bishoppes, greit Barrons and burgesses gif thair selis heirupon, to be usit, as sall be thought maist expedient be them, for the honor of the realme and securitie of the Noblemen, and otheris having entris in the caus.

JAMES, Regent.	ALEX. Lord HOME.
MORTON, Chancellar.	RUTHVEN.
GLENCARNE.	Lord SEMPILL.
ERROLL.	JOHN Lord GLAMISS.
BOWCHANE.	PATRICK Lord LINDESAY.
PAT. Lord GRAY.	JA. MAKGILL.
JOHN Lord GRAHAME.	HEN. BALNAVES.
UCHILTRIE.	W. MAITLAND.
INNERMEITH.	DRUMLANERK.
ADAM ORCHADEN.	CONINGHAMEHEID.
ROBERT, Commendatar of Dumferling.	JOHN ERSKYN of Dun.
	WM. KIRKALDY.
ALEXANDER, Commendatar of Culross.	Jo. WISHART of Petarro.
	JAMES HALYBURTON.
Sir JAM. BALFOUR.	CRAIGMILLAR.

II.

ACT OF PARLIAMENT, ANENT THE RETENTIOUN OF OUR SOVERANE LORDIS MOTHERIS PERSON.

ITEM, Anent the artickle proponit be the Erlis, Lordis, and uther Nobill-men, quha tuik armis at Carbarrie hill, upon the xv. day of Junii last bypast: And anent thair conveningis of befoir, and of the cause of the apprehensioun of the Quene mother to our Souverane Lord. And quhidder the saidis Nobill-men, and utheris quhilkis tuik armis of befoir hir said apprehensioun, and quhilkis joynit with thame, and assistit thame at that tyme, or ony wayis sensyne, hes done the dewtie of Nobillmen, gude and trew subjectis of this realme, and na wayis offendit, nor transgressit the lawis in that effect, or ony thing depending thairupon, outher preceding or following the samin. Our Soverane Lord, with avise of my Lord Regent, and thré Estatis, and haill body of this present parliament, hes fundin, declairit, and concludit, and be this present act findis, declairis, and concludis, that the cause and occasioun of the conventiounis and messageis of the saidis Erlis, Lordis, Nobill-men, Baronis, and utheris faithfull and trew subjectis, and consequentlie, thair taking of armis, and cuming to the fieldis with oppin and displayit banneris, and the cause and occasioun of the taking of the said Quenis person, upon the said xv. day of Junii last bypast, and halding and detening of the samin within the housis and fortalice of Lochlevin, continuallie sensyne, presentlie, and in all tyme cuming: And generallie all uther thingis inventit, spokin, writtin, or done be thame, or ony of thame to that effect, sen the tent day of Februar last bypast, upon the quhilk day umquhile Henry King, than the said Quenis lauchfull husband, and our Souverane Lord the Kingis derrest father, was tressonablie, schamefullie, and horriblie murthourit, unto the day and dait of this present act, and in all tymes to cum, tuiching the said Quene, and detening of hir person : That the cause, and all thingis dependand thairon, or that ony wayis may pertene thairto, the intromissioun, or disponing upon hir propertie, casualiteis, or quhatsumever thing pertening, or that ony ways mycht pertene to hir, wes in the said Quenis awin default, in sa far as, be divers hir previe letteris writtin halelie with hir awin hand, and send be hir to James sumtyme Erle of Bothwell, cheif executour of the said horribill murthour, as weill befoir the committing thairof as thairefter : And be hir ungodlie and dishonourabill proceding to ane pretendit mariage with him, suddandlie and unprovisitlie thairefter, it is maist certane, that scho was previe, airt and pairt, of the actual devise and deid of the foirnamit murthour of the King hir lauchfull husband, and father to our Soverane Lord, committit be the said James sumtyme Erle of Bothwell, his complices and partakeris ; And thairfoir justlie deservis quhatsumever hes bene done to hir in ony tyme bygaine, or that sal be usit towardis hir, for the said cause in tyme cuming, quhilk sal be usit be advise of the Nobilitie, in respect that our said Soverane Lordis mother, with the said James, sumtyme Erle of Bothwell, zeid about be indirect and colourit menis, to colour and hald back the knawledge of the treuth of the committaris of the said cryme. Zit all men in thair hartis was fullelie perswadit of the authouris and devysaris of that mischevous and unworthie fact, awaiting quhill God sould move the hartis of sum to enter in the querrell for revengeing of the samin. And in the mene tyme, ane greit pairt of the Nobilitie, upon just feir to be handlit, and demanit in semblabill maner, as the King had bene of befoir; persaving alswa the Quene sa thrall, and swa blindlie affectionat to the private appetyte of that tyrane, and that baith he and scho had conspyirit togidder sic horrible crueltie, being thairwith all garnissit with an cumpanie of ungodlie and vitious personis, reddy to accomplische all their unlauchfull commandementis, of quhome he had ane sufficient number, continuallie awaiting upon him, for the samin effect, all nobill and vertuous men abhorring thair tyrannie and cumpanie, bot cheiflie suspecting, that thay, quha had sa tressonablie put downe, and destroyit the father, sould mak the innocent Prince, his onlie sone, and the principall, and almost onlie confort, send be God to this afflictit natioun, to taist of the samin coup, as the mony inventit purposis to pas quhair he was, and alswa quhair the Nobillmen war in, be thair oppin confusioun gaif sufficient warning and declaratioun: Quhairthrow the saidis Erlis, Lordis, Barronis, and utheris faithfull and trew subjectis taking armis, or utherwyse qvhatsumever joyning, and assisting in the said actioun, and in the saidis conventiounis, displaying baneris, and cuming to the feildis, taking and retening of the Quenis person, asweill in tymes bypast, as heirefter, and all utheris that hes thairefter, or sall in ony time cuming adjoyne to thame, and all things done be thame, or ony of thame, tuicheing that cause, and all uther thingis depending thairon, or that ony wayis may appertene thairto, the intromissioun, or disponing upon hir propirtie, or casualiteis, or quhatsumever uther thingis pertening, or ony wayis mycht appertene to hir, was in default of hirself, and the said James sumtyme Erle of Bothwell, and be the horribill and cruell murther of our said Soverane Lordis umquhile derrest father, conspyrit, devysit, committit, conseilit and colourit be thame, and not condignelie puneist according to the laws. And that the saidis Erlis, Lordis, Barronis, and utheris trew and faithfull subjectis, convening at ony conventioun bygaine, and now presentlie efter the said murthour, for furthering of the tryell thairof; and als thay, and all utheris that war on the feildis, tuik armis, apprehendit, held, keipit or detenit, or presentlie haldis, keipis or detenis hir person, or sall thairefter, or that has joynit or assistit, or sall in ony tyme heirefter joyne to thame in that querrell, tuicheing the premissis, ar, war, and sall be innocent, fré, and acquyte of the samin, and of all actioun, and cause criminall and civill, that may be intentit or persewit aganis thame, or ony of thame thairfoir, in ony tyme cuming. And that ane pairt of the Thré Estatis foirsaidis, Prelatis, Bischopis, greit Barronis, and burgessis, gaif thair seillis thairupon, to be usit as sall be thocht maist expedient be thame, for the honour of the realme, and security of the Nobill-men, and utheris havand enteres in the said cause. And decernis this declaratioun to be na wayis prejudiciall to the issue of our Soverane Lordis mother, lauchfullie cumin of hir body, to succeid to the crowne of this realme, nor thair airis.

III.

THE JOURNALS OF THE PROCEEDINGS OF THE LORDS OF THE PRIVY COUNCIL OF ENGLAND, WITH SOME OF THE CHIEF OF THE NOBILITY, CALLED TO MEET WITH THEM AT HAMPTON-COURT, THE 14TH AND 15TH DAYS OF DECEMBER 1568.

Altered and interlined by Cecil.

Apud Hampton-court, die Martis xiv. Decembris 1568.

The Quene's Majesty commanded the Lords of her privy counsell to call unto them th' Erles of Northumberland, Westmorland, Shrewsbery, Worcester, Huntington and Warwyk, to whom being assembled with the said councell, was declared, That hir Majesty, according to hir declaration heretofore made unto them of the cause of their calling to hir presence, which was, as she should find cause, so to participat unto them, as being principall persons of the Nobility of hir realme, the state of the cause of the Quene of Scotts: So now also finding much tyme to be spent in the hearing of the same since their coming, and yet nevertheless as much done as possible was to be done within this time, and the matter at some staye, by meanes that the Quene of Scotts Commissioners have refused any more conference: Hir Majesty thought good, not knowing how by common report they might be therof informed, to let them understand truly and playnly the state of the same, as herein making them her Counsellors, specially to keep the same secret to themselves, without prejudicing of the one part or the other, by any final opinion or determination to be conceived with themselves: Which as hir Majesty ment to observe for hir self, so would she gladly have it observed by them. Which intention of hir Majestie being declared unto the said Lords, they all thanked hir Majesty for this hir favourable goodnes so to esteme of them, and promised to observe hir Majesty's direction, both in the secrecy, and in the suspension of their judgments.

This being done, the whole procedings of the Commissioners, first at York, and next at Westminster, untill the last session ended at Westminster about the 10th of this month, was to them sommarely declared and repeated: Wherin, besides many circumstances tending to make demonstration of the sincerity of the Quene's Majesty and hir Commissioners, there was briefly shewed unto them, how the Quene of Scotts Commissioners first accused the Erle of Murray and his colleagues, being now in commission for, and in the name of James King of Scotts: And how they did therto make answer, by justification of themselves by the lawes of the realme, without any special depraving or calumniating the honour of the Quene; and next thereto, the replication of the other party. And furder was declared, how herupon the same treaty and conference, upon reasonable causes, was removed to Westminster; and in what sort the same conference was there revived; and how the Erle of Murray and his colleagues, being charged to answer the replication, after protestation made, were unwilling to procede any furder to touch the name and honor of the Quene, if their adversaries had not pressed them with lack of loyalty. For remedy wherof they produced by way of addition to their first answear, wherin they avowed, That as the Erle Bothwell was the executor of the murder, so was the Quene of Scotts a procurer and deviser of the said murder. And after this was likewise declared unto the said Erles, acording to the several memorials therof already made and put in writing, the acts passed in all the former sessions at Westminster: For the more perfect declaration of all which said acts, there was first produced a writing in manner of articles, which was exhibited to the Commissioners the 6th of December, as appears in the memorial of that session.

And before those articles were read, there were produced sundry lettres written in French, supposed to be written by the Quene of Scotts own hand, to the Erle Bothwell; and therwith also one long sonnet; and a promise of marriage in the name of the said Quene with the said Erle Bothwell. Of which lettres the originals, supposed to be written with the Quene of Scotts own hand, were then also presently produced and perused; and being read, were duly conferred and compared, for the manner of writing and fashion of orthography, with sundry other lettres long since heretofore written, and sent by the said Quene of Scotts to the Quene's Majesty. And next after these was produced and read a declaration of the Erle Morton, of the manner of the finding of the said lettres, as the same was exhibited upon his oath the 9th of December: In collation wherof no difference was found. Of all which lettres and writings the true copies are contained in the memorial of the acts of the sessions of the 7th and 8th of December.

And after this were also produced and read the examination of John Haye the younger of Tallowe, and of John Hepborne, and George Dalglys, who were executed at Edinburgh for the said murder, which be conteyned amongst the acts of the session of the 8th of December. And next after that was read the confession and deposition of Thomas Crawfurd, conteyned amongst the writings of the 9th of December.

And forasmuch as the night approached, it was thought good to differ the furder declaration of the rest untill the nixt day following.

IV.

Die Mercurii, xv. Decembris 1568.

The Lords of the privy counsell having the Erles before mentioned with them, declared, That where yesterday mention and report was made of a book of articles being divided into five parts, they shuld also see and heare the same book, and so the same was thoroughly and distinctly read unto them. And after the same was produced and read, the deposition of one William Powry, one of the four that was executed at Edinburgh, as the same deposition was exhibited the 8th of December. Next wherunto was produced, read and viewed, the original writing, supposed to be written by the Erle of Huntley, being a Contract of mariage betwixt the Quene and the Erle Bothwell, dated at Seaton the 5th of Aprill, and subscribed by the Quene and the Erle Bothwell with their own proper handes, as was alledged: The true copy wherof is amongst the things exhibited the 7th of December. After this was also produced and read the extract of the arraynment and deliverance of the Erle Bothwell, by an assise, at Edinburgh the 12th of April 1567, according to the copy thereof, being amongst the writings exhibited the 7th of December. Nixt after this was also produced, read and viewed, a writing subscribed, dated the 10th of this month of December, subscribed by the Erle of Murray and his colleagues, to testify the former writings produced, as written by the said Quene of Scotts, to be hir own hand-writing. Which also is to be seen amongst the writings exhibited to the Commissioners the 12th of December.

There was also produced and read a writing of another deposition of Thomas Crawfurd, upon his oath exhibited to the Commissioners the 13th of December, concerning certen answers made to him by the foresaid John Hepborne and John Haye, upon the scaffold in Edinburgh, instantly before their execution.

There was also produced, read and shewed to them, the form and manner of the holding of the parliament at Edinburgh the 15th of December 1567, wherin the numbers of the three Estates were there expressed, and alledged to be as great an assembly of the said estates, as had been any time by the space of one hundred years before: Which writing also is conteyned amongst the rest exhibited the 9th of December.

There was also report made unto them of an act of parliament made at the same time, conteyning the confirmation of the dimission of the crown by the Quene of

Scotts, and of the coronation of hir sonne, and of the regency in the person of the Erle of Murray. At which parliament hath bene alledged, that the Erles of Huntley and Argile, and the Lord Herrys, did acknowledge the same authorities: And for that purpose, as a writing was produced before the Commissioners the 8th of December, to prove the same, so was the same writing read this present day; which writing is amongst others exhibited the said 8th day.

Besides the production, reading and shewing of these sundry kinds of writings here before mentioned, considering the length of time that was spent in the reading the foresaid writings, many of them being of great length, there was a short and just report made of sundry other matters which were exhibited to the said Commissioners, as the same may plainly appear amongst the acts of the severall sessions of the said Commissioners at Westminster; as, the acts of the two severall divorces, which are of great length in writing, and the acts of parliament for the attaynder of all the persons charged with the murder. And it is to be noted, that at the time of the producing, shewing and reading of all these foresaid writings, there was no special choyse nor regard had to the order of the producing therof, but the whole writings lying altogether upon the counsel table, the same were one after an other showed rather by hap, as the same did ly upon the table, than with any choyse made, as by the natures therof, if time had so served, might have been. And in the end it was said unto the said Erles, that in this sort they were now made participant of the whole state of the cause, even as largely as the rest of hir Majestie's Privy Counsel were: And therfore they were newly again required to have in remembrance hir

Majestie's first charge to have the same kept in secret by them as hir Counsellors in this cause. And that where the Quene of Scotts Commissioners being made privy of this the accusation of the said Quene, have forborn to answer to the same, and refused also to have any furder conference in this matter, pressing only to have the Quene their Mistris permitted to come to the presence of the Quene's Majestie to make her answer, and otherwise to make no answer at all; it hath been considered by her Majestie, and not thought unmeet, in this sort following, to answer the said Commissioners, if they shall persist in the said request: That hir Majestie will be very willing and desirous, that some good answer may be made by the said Quene, either by her Commissioners and delegates, or by her own self, before such sufficient persons as her Majestie would send to her: But considering her Majestie had at her first coming into the realm, found it not mete for her own honour to have her, being so commonly defamed of so horrible crimes, to come to her presence, before she might be therof some wise purged, so also now the crimes, wherewith she hath been by common fame burdened, being by many vehement allegations and presumptions, upon things now produced, made more apparent, she can not, without manifest blemish of hir own honour, in the sicht of the world, agree to have the same Q. to cum into hir presence, untill the said horrible crimes may be by sum just and reasonable answer avoidit and removit from hir, which hir Majestie would wish might also be.

And in this sort hir Majesty's intention being opened to the said Erlis, in presence of the said privy council, the said Erlis severally made answer; First acknowledging themselves much bound unto hir Majestie, that it had pleased hir to impart to them the stait of this great cause, in so plain manner, as they did perceive it; wherin they had sene such foul matteris, as they thought truly, in their consciences, That hir Majestie had just cause herein given to make to the said commissioners such ane answer, being as reasonable as the case might bear; and the rather for that they could not allow it as meet for hir Majestie's honour to admit the said Q. to hir Majestie's presence, as the case now did stand.

www.ingramcontent.com/pod-product-compliance
Lightning Source LLC
Chambersburg PA
CBHW020921230426
43666CB00008B/1523